Twisted

Twisted

My Dreadlock Chronicles

Bert Ashe

BOLDEN
AN AGATE IMPRINT
CHICAGO

Portions of this book originally appeared as "Invisible Dread," in *Blackberries and Redbones: Critical Articulations of Black Hair/Body Politics in Africana Communities*. (Cresskill, NY: Hampton Press, 2010.)

The author gratefully acknowledges permission to reprint lines from "For the Jim Crow Mexican Restaurant in Cambridge, Massachusetts Where My Cousin Esteban Was Forbidden to Wait Tables Because He Wears Dreadlocks," from *A Mayan Astronomer in Hell's Kitchen: Poems by Martin Espada*. Copyright © 2001 by Martin Espada. Reprinted by permission of W. W. Norton and Company, Incorporated.

Printed in the United States of America

Library of Congress Cataloging-in-Publication Data

Ashe, Bert.
Twisted : my dreadlock chronicles / Bert Ashe.
pages cm
Summary: "A personal account of an African-American professor's mid-life experiences when he decides to grow dreadlocks, with a cultural and political history of dreadlocks"--Provided by publisher.
ISBN 978-1-932841-96-1 (paperback) -- ISBN 1-932841-96-2 (paperback)
1. Dreadlocks. 2. Hairdressing of African Americans. 3. Hairstyles--Social aspects--United States. 4. Beauty, Personal--Social aspects--United States. 5. Ashe, Bert. 6. African American men--Race identity. 7. African American men--Social conditions. I. Title.
GT2295.U5A74 2015
391.5--dc23

2014040169

10 9 8 7 6 5 4 3 2 1

Bolden is an imprint of Agate Publishing. Agate books are available in bulk at discount prices. For more information, go to agatepublishing.com.

For my friend Gerald Brown—who would have fully understood

Contents

Hair issues are among us. We must tease them out, hold them up to the light, and coax them into art.

—Lisa Jones, *Bulletproof Diva: Tales of Race, Sex and Hair*

Confession (i)

I killed dreadlocks. It was a crime of passion.

Anyone with eyes can see how dread has spread. If a map of the United States is the country's headshot in profile, then California is a snub nose, lower Texas is a double chin, and the Great Lakes are three stubby blue dreads sprouting out of an American scalp—with a thick Florida dreadlock dangling beneath the nation's neckline. If the hairstyle has become less radical, if it's devolved in the last decade or so, dropping from exclusive, Uppercase Dreads to common-denominator, lowercase locks, point fingers directly at me. I walk around campus, cheer at ball games, joke with my kids; I sit at movies, dine at restaurants, worship at church; I live and breathe under black, lipstick-thick tubes of hair that curl out of my head and slide down around my neck and shoulders.

God knows I'd always wanted dreadlocks. Wanted them for the longest time. And, finally, I did it: I got twisted. And it was everything I'd wanted it to be, as well as nothing I'd ever expected. I loved and dreaded dreads. They both satisfied my curiosity and caused me, at times, to be sure I was losing my mind.

The killing was unintentional. But I'm confessing, nevertheless, freely admitting to it, intentional or not. You could call it involuntary manslaughter, if you prefer. I call it murder. "But that's getting too far ahead of the story, almost to the end, although the end is in the beginning and lies far ahead," to quote Mr. Ralph Ellison, an idiomatic spirit who hovers above my head and breathes down my neck, a man whose derisive laughter I can hear at any waking moment of the day or night...

Hair varies, after all. Superman and *Thriller*-era Michael Jackson have two of the more famous locks of hair-dangling-over-foreheads. But their locks each look slightly different. People use the term "a lock of hair" as if they're sure they know what that means, but there's no true consensus. All those individual mental images of a lock, in all those various minds, are all slightly different—and sometimes significantly different. "Lock" is a deceptively simple term, since the look of an exact lock of hair cannot be strictly determined. A dreadlock? Even less so.

What you're about to read is a dread simulation; it takes the form of a single, heavy dreadlock. The narrative strands weave as tightly as the hair fibers that lock locks together: History ducks and overlaps with culture; the process of locking hair wraps up and around questions of identity; public perception winds down and around racial issues that turn up and curve and twirl—and it all weaves in and out and around examinations of the nature of style itself. What follows is not linear, cannot be linear—because dreadlocks are not a linear hairstyle.

Think back to the first time you saw dreadlocks, back when they were still alive. It was such a stylistic disruption from the familiar black hairstyles of the day, even the "natural" black hairstyles of the day. Consciously or unconsciously, apprehending a head of dread forces the viewer to recalibrate what a hairstyle is supposed to be, is supposed to mean. Do the same when you read on.

You'll see: I was sure I'd killed dreadlocks, once and for all time. I just knew that in thirty years the style would be endlessly mocked and ridiculed, parodically worn for ironic effect, the same way the Afro is worn today. (I don't know who killed the Afro, and I don't care—that's someone else's burden.) It's painful. I loved dreadlocks long before I wore them, loved whatever I imagined they stood for, loved everything I thought they were supposed to mean.

I thought it was all over. I had no idea.

Origins

Intentionality (i)

Someone invented fire. Surely, at first, someone *discovered* it, but the building of an intentional fire?—so that it can be relied upon?—someone invented that. Someone invented drawing. And drumming. Some nameless human somewhere, during the prehistoric era, standing with hands on hips, head quizzically cocked to the side, must have muttered some grunt-filled version of "Hmmmmm," and thought, if not said aloud, "What if I tried... *this*?"

A long, long time ago, someone invented dreadlocks. And then the people around that person reacted to the style. Might have been, "I like that," which spurred the wearer to continue; might have been, "I hate that"—which, perhaps, spurred the wearer to defiantly continue.

Either way, *somebody* invented dreadlocks—the recognizable style. But who? I'm guessing someone saw matted hair and it triggered a feeling of aesthetic pleasure, and that person figured out a way to duplicate that accident for themselves. Clearly, someone recognized dreadlocks as a distinctive "style," but whoever that was—and exactly when—is unrecorded.

Cutting—styling—had to come first. In order to "let" hair grow, a culture of cutting would already have to be in place. Once that culture of cutting was set, *then* one could cut, or let hair grow, resulting from some sort of aesthetic desire. Think of beards. On most men, facial hair simply grows. But for a population of men who decide to "let" their beards grow, the cutting of beards had to come before allowing-to-grow became an intentional stylistic option.

So. Let's get it straight, as it were: first came hair. Then, over time, came the styling of hair: cutting and shaping. And then, it would follow, came the "allowing-to-grow" option—leaving hair uncut, leaving hair unshaped—which slowly emerged as a stylistic possibility once the culture of cutting had set the aesthetic boundaries in the first place.

Going Outside (i)

On Monday morning, March 9, 1998, I stood in front of my bathroom mirror, looking for dreadlocks. I'd been searching for a long time; I'd been seeking them out, trying to talk to them, bargain with them, reason with them. Dreadlocks dropped between my eyes and the world like night-vision goggles fastened over the eyes of a soldier on patrol. I couldn't help seeing the world through an infrared, black hair prism. It was like a prolonged hallucination; black peoples' heads—and the hair upon them—were blown up to quadruple scale, and as they walked the earth their bodies and faces melted, and all I could see, all that mattered, was their hair. My eyes would tear and fog, and when they cleared, I would blearily zoom in on black hair in general or dreadlocks in particular—and I absolutely had no off switch, either, any more than one could imagine a day without weather. It didn't matter where I was, who I was with, what time of day it was, or what I was doing—the intensity with which I studied and observed and contemplated black hair sometimes made my head hurt.

I stood there, staring at my head in the mirror. Every now and then fast-motion-photography hair would shoot out, morphing my near-baldie into a thicket, into bushy locks, into a head of hair you could lose a hand in. On that second

Monday of March in 1998, I decided I wasn't going to cut my hair again for a long, long time. I said it aloud, my mirror image forming the words as the sound broke bathroom silence: "I'm growing dreadlocks."

The words changed nothing. No sudden darkness as clouds passed in front of the sun; no rumbling, ominous music slowly emerging from underneath the scene. I simply said it aloud, and then said it again. "I'm growing dreadlocks." No one knew. And no one would guess. As short as my hair was, the idea that I was growing dreadlocks would seem as absurd as an asthmatic fat boy insisting he was going to run the marathon. My hair was longer than it had been a couple of weeks earlier, but it was still very, very short. When I stood in the bathroom and blinked and my hair shrank back to reality, I laughed at the notion. Dreadlocks? Me? Please.

• • •

I wanted to go outside. I'd tried to get outside for years, I really had. I cultivated an appetite for rock music in college, and I loved going to art movies at Camera One in downtown San Jose. I drove into and hung out in San Francisco and Berkeley as often as I could. Once, in the early 80s, my across-the-dorm-hallway friend Yvonne and I went to San Francisco to see an indie movie called *Smithereens*, Susan Seidelman's first feature. Standing in line, I felt like I was finally with my people: emaciated-looking guys in skinny black jeans and Day-Glo Chuck Taylors, girls with spiky, magenta hair, black dudes in torn Clash tees. I felt like just hanging out in line, just being on the scene, took me outside a little bit. I hated the movie, but that's beside the point. Sitting in that theater, feeling "in" among outcasts, watching similar outcasts onscreen, with me in my own scruffy tee and hole-at-both-knees jeans, I felt slightly... "out." After the movie, as Yvonne and I walked down the street away from the theater, I spied a black woolen scarf on the sidewalk, scooped it up, and wrapped it around my neck. I lost that same scarf about five years later in a mosh pit at a Fishbone concert at Rockitz in Richmond,

Virginia. I always thought there was some poetry there, in the way that scarf floated toward me—and in the way that scarf floated away from me.

I wanted to go outside. See, yes, it's absolutely true that I'm the son of a hardworking man who for years was a teacher and then principal in the Los Angeles Unified School District; I'm the son of a woman who was a special education teacher in that same district. I did grow up in Harbor City, in Los Angeles County, and I did play in my cul-de-sac, like that kid from *The Wonder Years*, on a street whose households were like a mini-United Nations: Mexican, Chinese, Japanese, German, Italian, African American, and, of course, WASP, all on one multi-culti street, and we all played well with each other and let's all link hands and sing along, shall we? Because I don't want to anymore. Yes, yes, I went to Nathaniel Narbonne High School and lived in a subdivision called, of all things, the Palo del Amo Woods—with nary a naturally grown tree in sight: Cub Scouts, YMCA, tennis lessons, piano lessons, swimming lessons, accordion lessons, summer camp, Pee Wee football, alto saxophone in junior high school band, tenor saxophone in Los Caballeros Youth Band, and high school band. High school basketball. Student government, class president in elementary and junior high, student body president in junior high, graduation speaker in high school and every other graduation that I had up through high school—are you sick yet? Queasy? Well, it's true. It's all true. I was completely engaged. I was raised to be an achiever, a little brown suburban robot: totally plugged in. It's what I knew, and I knew as much as I could; I bought "in," and I bought "it"—I bought it all.

It really wasn't until I went away to school and met some hard-core brothers from the streets—and some real-deal bohemians—that I realized what I'd missed, that I'd been cocooned growing up in a way that I simply didn't understand before. How could I know? I guess that's what "sheltered" means: not just protected, but blinkered. Capped. Shuttered.

• • •

As the years went by I grew up in those Palo del Amo Woods, those vanilla, Spielbergian suburbs. My body expanded, lengthened, and jutted away from earth in those suburbs where I lived. But inside, deep inside, I just knew I'd grown up in Berkeley, attended Berkeley High, kicked around Telegraph Avenue as the son of radical, militant professors. Inside my rib cage, my beating heart told me that I'd grown up in Greenwich Village, slouching around CBGBs in the East Village, meeting my pal Jean-Michel Basquiat for coffee at a cafe at the corner of Bleecker and MacDougal, the son of an herbalist and a jazz musician. Or maybe I'd grown up in Cambridge, Massachusetts, a Harvard Square veteran, the son of an artist—and an experimental novelist.

See, then I wouldn't have had to get outside myself. I'd have had matching selves—the same one on the inside as the one on the outside. As is, I was this Dark Stranger, this outcast on the inside, but all the world could see was the obliging, adroit façade, the Universal Negro: good guy Bert. But that's not quite right, either, because I am that good guy, too! I absolutely am that; I wouldn't want to lose that. It's real. It's Me. I just wanted to figure out a way I could come closer to finding the perfect green bubble in the middle of the level bar, achieving that delicate, ideal, teeter-totter balance between the Me I felt myself to be, and the Me I seemed to be to those who could see me. I wondered, *Dreadlocks, can you do that for me?*

Art, Science, Religion (i)

Homo habilis, the first species of the genus *Homo*, lived in South and East Africa about two million years ago. They possessed some rough tools, mainly to extract meat from dead animals. But *Homo erectus* had a larger brain, and it's around this time that hand axes began to appear. Could *Homo erectus* have even been bothered to use the hand axe to cut his or her hair? I doubt it. My belief, based purely on common sense, mixed with some brief and scattered examples of camping as a kid with Cub Scouts and my family, is that they had far more to worry about keeping their stomachs full than styling hair. Steven Mithen, who has tracked the development of the human mind, agrees with me; he calls the world of the *Homo neanderthalensis* "tedious, with the same set of tools being used for narrow purposes and with no hint in the archaeological evidence of art, science, or religion."

And what is hairstyling, at least in the black community, but a telling combination of artistic expression, an almost scientific approach to dealing with kinks, and a nearly obsessive devotion to the collaborative styling process that borders on the religious: an art, a science, and a religion. By the time *Homo sapiens* evolved, not only were the dead regularly buried, boats built, and cave walls painted, but people began, about 5,000 years ago, to decorate their bodies with beads and pendants. They also began to cut and style their hair. And it's at this moment that men and women can choose to *opt out* of the developing social norms by such gestures as styling their hair—or, rather, refusing to style their hair—in ways that might well frighten, or provoke "dread," in the prevailing culture. The hairstyle we call dreadlocks would do that, I would imagine, if for no other reason than its harkening back to the days when hair was merely "stuff" emerging from bodies.

Inscrutability (i)

My secret lasted exactly 24 hours. My wife, Valerie, is the love of my life, the mother of my children, all that's good in my world; she also has always had senses working overtime. I walked into the kitchen of our colonial house on a bright spring morning the day after I'd spent so much time in the mirror. She glanced at me, looked away, then ripped back for a double take. She said, "You know what? You need a haircut. Bad. What's going on?" In my head, I was smug; I thought, *This is happening exactly the way you expected it, Bert. Tell her you're letting it grow.* "I'm letting it grow out," I said carelessly, casually opening the refrigerator.

"Does it have to look so scruffy?" she said. Val and I make a curious pair. We're both around the same age, both college educated, both love to read, both hold similar views on morals and character. But our differences are stark and plain to see. She was from a military family, I was from an education family. I was raised in Southern California, her home base was in Southern Virginia. Practical and warm, clear-eyed and direct, Val was often the commonsensical voice of reason to my wild and risky ideas. If I was Sputnik, prone to soaring flights in outer space, Val was an earthen garden, feet planted firmly on the ground. That morning she'd barely begun to suggest ways I could grow my hair out more gracefully when the morning carnival drowned out any possible conversation. My athletic, three-year-old son, Garnet, as subtle as a swinging sledgehammer, needed his shoes tied; my daughter, Jordan, a lithe, graceful seven-year-old, was loudly loading her backpack before I took them to daycare and to school.

A little while later Val and I were on our way to Boston. As I pointed the car east on the Massachusetts Turnpike, she turned to me and said, apropos of absolutely nothing, "Are you growing dreadlocks?"

I was shocked into silence for a moment or two. Then I came clean. What else could I do? "Yes," I said, grimly.

She smiled and nodded. She'd always liked the style.

"But now, Val," I said, "how could you have possibly gotten from 'You need a haircut' back at the house to 'Are you growing dreadlocks?' now? What exactly was the road you traveled in your head to get here?"

She just smiled her inscrutable smile. Conversation drifted elsewhere—we had business in Boston, and we focused on that. But the secret was out, even though I hadn't volunteered anything. I didn't mention the other issues I'd been thinking about. I'd have to figure those out for myself.

Dreaming David Letterman

Here's what passed for sleeping late on a Saturday morning in the spring of 1998: Jordan solemnly standing next to the bed, asking if she can watch a "movie" (*Yes*); Garnet bounding past her onto the bed, asking for candy (*No*); either Jordan, who also then leaps onto the bed, or Garnet—or both, simultaneously—shrieking, "He hit me"/"*She* hit *me*!"

I'm one of those unfortunates who have one shot at sleep, particularly in the morning. Once I wake up, I'm up. So I would try to rope-a-dope the sleep gods when the kids invaded by keeping my voice low, barely slitting my eyes, and insisting to myself that I was still drowsy even as I issued commands and settled disputes.

In between interruptions, I dreamed that I was inside a control booth, mere inches from the director and the switcher, at the CBS television studios in New York City…

Ready Camera Two for Paul…

[laughter] … Now say hello to my good friend *Mr. Paul Shaffer.*

Take *Camera Two! Ready Camera One on Dave … wait for music out …* ***take*** *Camera One! We'll be switching between them—stay ready.…*

[seated, shuffling cards, sipping coffee] So Paul, how ya doin' tonight?

[standing behind keyboard, gripping microphone, hair seeming to recede even as we watch] Um, just fine, Dave, I really think so.

Youuuuu *think* so.

Um, yeah, Dave.

You *think* so?

Uh, well, I *thought* so, anyway. Now I'm not so sure.…

Well, now, *Pauuul…* Don't *not* think so on *my* account.… *Aw, heh heh.* Hell with it, Paul, let's go straight to tonight's Top Ten List, okay? [wild applause]

Ready graphics? Ready Camera Two on Paul? ***Take*** *graphics!* ***Take*** *Two! … Ready Camera One on Dave? Annnnd…* ***Take*** *One!*

Paul, do you think it'd be "*fine*" if I did tonight's Top Ten List now?

Sure, Dave.

Thank you, Paul. [in a mock-disgusted, muttered aside, Dave repeats] "I *think* so…" Okay, tonight's Top Ten List is "The Top Ten Things Bert Ashe Should Say When People Ask Him Why His Hair Is So Long!" [raucous, sustained, roof-raising applause greets his words; Dave has to wait what seems like two or three *minutes* before continuing. Just as the audience reaction is subsiding, a huge six-foot-by-eight-foot photo of Bert slowly scrolls down into view next to Dave, hovering over the empty guest seats. In Bert's photographic image, his increasingly longer hair is wild and uncombed; he has a puzzled, confused, duh-is-that-a-camera? look on his face. The audience reacts by screaming even louder. Finally Dave continues, smacking the cards on the desk repeatedly in barely repressed delight as he says]

Okay, here we go. The…

Top Ten Things Bert Ashe Should Say When People Ask Him Why His Hair Is So Long!

Ready Camera Three on drummer; ***take*** *Three! Okay, ready Camera One on Dave…* ***take*** *One!*

Number *Ten*: "I had a 70s flashback, and when I realized I was still in the 90s I decided to just go with it." [laughter]

Number Nine: "I lost my clippers?" [mild titters]

Number Eight: "Who says Denzel in *He Got Game* gets to have all the fun?" [laughter]

Num-ber Se-ven: "Yo *mama* like it this way." [whoops and applause; as it dies down, Dave cracks] Did you hear that, Paul? "Yo *Ma*ma *like* it this way!" Heh, heh, heh—You *think* so—?!

Dammit! Camera Two, ***take*** *Paul's reaction; Camera One, stay on Dave;* ***Take*** *two! Ready graphics…* ***take*** *graphics!*

Number *Six*: "It's performance art, and now you're a part of the show." [mild laughter]

Nnnnnnnnnumber Five: "Two words: 'Linc Hayes.'" [half laughter; half baffled silence] Paul, didja ever watch *The Mod Squad*?

Take *Camera One on Dave! Ready Camera Two on Paul;* ***take*** *Camera Two! Ready Camera One…*

Yes, I did, Dave. Peggy Lipton was fabulous, just fabulous!

Take *Camera One!*

Never mind, Paul. Num-ber *Four*: "'Cause it's *my hair*, you idiot—I just *feel* like it!" [wild applause; Dave pauses, then continues]

Number Three: "I decided I would slap the twenty-first pinhead that mentioned it—guess which number you are?" [big laughter]

Nummer*two*: "I'm studying to be a Black Panther—once I perfect this time machine, I'm *outta* here!" [laughs]

And the Number One Thing Bert Ashe Should Say When People Ask Him Why His Hair Is So Long: "I wanted to rap with the Afros, but I didn't want to wear a wig!" [applause, music out]

I have no idea where things went from there; Garnet interrupted me, wanting something, and I never went back to that dream….

Going Outside (ii)

How do you know the right time? For much of my undergraduate years at San Jose State, beginning in 1977, I didn't wear a hairstyle—I wore a white hat, a lot like Gilligan's hat in *Gilligan's Island*, and I wore it all the time; if you saw me, you saw the hat. And although I was aware dreadlocks existed, I didn't actively consider them a stylistic option. Dreadlocks, alas, simply wasn't a conscious possibility for me at that time. What I couldn't know was that, for years to come, I would have regular dread-growing possibilities tantalizingly dangled in front of me, and I would reach out, would flail about, but ultimately fail to launch the locks.

The first time I seriously considered growing dreadlocks was 1983, while I was working as a disc jockey at KBCE-FM in Alexandria, Louisiana. I was a bit older then, somewhere around age 24, and I actively wanted them. I had a little more awareness—I knew they were important to the Rastafarians—but I didn't know much more than that. I was attracted to the style, and so I considered it, even though I knew less than nothing about how to go about it.

But as fate would have it, I briefly dated a Jamaican woman in Louisiana. And when I told her I was getting locks, she talked me out of it. Honestly, I wonder if, even though I wanted to do it, I was actively looking for an excuse not to do it, and for me to now say "she talked me out of it" is, perhaps, displacing the blame for why I didn't do it then. Nevertheless, her argument was that it was wrong for non-Rastas to wear locks, that it was sacrilegious, that it would be a massive cultural insult to Rastas everywhere. Rastafarians took a solemn Nazarite vow not to cut their hair, she said. Rastas wore dreadlocks as an important aspect of their religious faith, and to lock my hair, since I had no connection to Rastafarianism, would be, in her view, to do it for stylistic purposes only. "Fashion dread" is the term I've heard Rastas use since, and even though she didn't use those words exactly, that was her point. "Please don't do it, Bert," she urged one day at the radio studio, touching my hand, looking deeply into my eyes.

Well. *How do you know the right time?* Apparently, that wasn't it. I don't want to believe that her urgings were the reason—I want to believe that it was just not something I was ready to do. I want to believe that, given my stylistic acumen at the time—and the fact that I barely *had* a "stylistic acumen" at the time—I wasn't nearly ready to make such a drastic move, whether or not I had ever even met her, but the fact remains: No matter how much her words actually did count, whether her urgings were foundational or merely the basis for my own pathetic excuse not to do it, I didn't grow dreadlocks. Locks remained on my radar screen, but the blip faded and beeped with far less urgency for about six years.

By 1989 I was an English graduate student at Virginia Commonwealth University, and my closest buddies in the program were three other black students: Agymah, Ronica, and Erika. Two of them wore dreadlocks, and the clicking and beeping on my dread radar intensified once again. Our little black grad quartet met often, and I had a lot of time to study Erika's and Agymah's dreadlocks. Erika's were thick, luscious, and shoulder length, as I recall, and Agymah's were thinner and longer, although he would gradually, relentlessly twist the smaller ones into larger ones over the years I knew him. If there was a genesis of my "lock lust," my desire for a particular lock "look," it might well have occurred as the four of us would regularly meet for coffee or beer, in graduate seminars, in school hallways, or at the meetings of a local black writer's group. Any time I saw them, I was "all in" their hair. I'm not sure I talked about it much at the time, but both their heads remained vividly alive in my eyes and my consciousness.

And I still didn't get locked. And I know why: It would have felt too imitative, I thought. It would have had too much of the "me, too" about it. *How do you know the right time?* This didn't feel like it. It would have felt less like my own idea, and more like an idea that I'd latched onto, based on my friends' hair, both of whom had arrived in Richmond already wearing dreadlocks. At least, that was what I told myself, anyway.

I have no conscious recollection of actively desiring dreadlocks while I attended William and Mary, studying for my doctorate in American Studies beginning in 1991. I don't recall thinking overtly about dreadlocks when I went on the academic job market. I began as an assistant professor in the English department at the College of the Holy Cross in the fall semester of 1996, but before I went north I attended a Paul Beatty fiction reading on June 17, 1996, in Washington, DC, and he tellingly inscribed my copy of *The White Boy Shuffle* this way: "Bert, good luck. Don't let New England get you down." He already knew what I was about to find out: Climactically—and culturally—New England was the polar opposite of anywhere I had lived before. I'd grown up and gone to college on the West Coast, and then spent nearly fifteen years in the south. Moving to Worcester, Massachusetts, was unlike anything I'd ever experienced before.

I loved my colleagues at Holy Cross. "New England" wasn't their fault, and it also wasn't their fault that their warmth couldn't counteract the chill in the region. In their own way they did everything they could to ease the transition. But crusty, grouchy, cranky New England is what it is, after all, and I struggled to come to grips with living in my new home, particularly since Val and the kids stayed in Richmond my first year at the school while I finished my dissertation. Was race a factor? Of course. Race is always a factor, in everything. But I'm also aware that people of all races can move to New England and get rocked, get destabilized by the provincial peculiarities of the region.

It didn't happen right away, and I don't recall exactly how it happened, but gradually I began to think that perhaps *this* was the right time to get locked. After being aware, hyper aware, critically aware, of dreadlocks for better than twenty years, dancing close to locking, stumbling away from locking, barely thinking about locking, then slouching toward locking yet again, I had, over the years, somehow actually matured into someone who could make the decision for myself, regardless of what anyone else told me I should consider, or how it might look to people who surely wouldn't have cared what I did with my hair in any case.

I'm pretty sure I would eventually have gotten locked no matter where my first academic job was, but since I only landed in New England, I'll never know. I think, however, that at least part of why I actually, finally wanted to grow dreadlocks is that I urgently wanted to create some space for myself; I wanted to make a statement to myself and for myself, and I didn't want to say it aloud: I wanted my hair to talk for me. And this time I was old enough and wise enough and centered enough to finally give myself permission to do what I'd long wanted to do: to go outside. I didn't have to ask myself *How do you know the right time?* I think the answer is that when it's truly the right time you don't have to ask—or answer—that question. It was just time. Period. And I knew it.

American Joker

Two random men, plucked from the American maelstrom by Ralph Waldo Ellison, both wearing striking hats, one with remarkable hair.

While walking in Harlem beside Riverside Park one sunny Sunday afternoon in the mid-1970s, Ellison observed a young man who parked on the sidewalk "in a shiny new blue Volkswagen Beetle decked out with a gleaming Rolls-Royce radiator." The flow of strollers apparently came to a halt as the man emerged from his elaborately enhanced Bug. He possessed, writes Ellison in "The Little Man at Chehaw Station," "something of that magical cornucopian combustion by which a dozen circus clowns are exploded from an even more miniaturized automobile. Looming as tall as a professional basketball center, he unfolded himself and stretched to his full imposing height."

According to Ellison, the man wore "handsome black riding boots" along with "fawn-colored riding breeches of English tailoring" and a "dashy dashiki" as he wielded a leather riding crop—all the while wearing "a black homburg hat tilted at a jaunty angle" that "floated majestically on the crest of his huge Afro-coiffed head."

As Ellison watched, the man pulled out a "Japanese single-lens reflex camera," positioned it carefully, and activated its self-timer. Then, writes Ellison, "with a ballet leap across the walk, he assumed a position beside his car. There he rested his elbow upon its top, smiled, and gave himself sharp movie director's commands as to the desired poses, then began taking a series of self-portraits. This done, he placed the camera upon the hood of his Volkswagen and took another series of self-shots in which, manipulating a lengthy ebony cigarette holder, he posed himself in various fanciful attitudes against the not-too-distant background of the George Washington Bridge. All in all, he made a scene to haunt one's midnight dreams and one's noon repose."

Role model number one.

Nearly fifteen years later, strolling that same piece of Riverside Drive in Harlem—this time on a Wednesday, on May 23, 1990—Ellison spotted "a tall young brown-skinned man" who was "carrying himself with a proud military bearing subtly combined with a subdued version of Harlem strut." Ellison recorded his encounter with the young man in some notes he compiled for a talk at Columbia University. But it wasn't the man's walk that attracted Ellison's attention. "Nor was it the grim set of his features. But when we were face to face," writes Ellison, "and I looked up to see that he was wearing a gray cap which bore the insignia of the Confederate Army, I was flabbergasted. It was as though the most tragic incident in American history had leaped from a New York sidewalk to confound me with a transformation of the color symbolism which had ignited the Civil War.

"'So you've joined the Confederacy,' I managed to sputter, to which tentative question there was only a grim look of reply.

"The young man continued his march and I continued mine, but then I paused, looked back, and there he was, hands on hips, Confederate-capped head thrown back, bubbling with uncontrollable laughter."

Role model number two.

I'm framing Confederate Cap-man, making sure he's properly placed. I want him standing tall, right beside the culture-clashed young man Ellison encountered a decade and a half earlier. Let them both pose for the camera; they'd make a marvelous pair. Ellison is a cultural observer skilled at making sense of the world he sees as he walks American streets. He erects—and then employs—an American cultural context to understand both encounters with both men: Of the latter, the Confederate Cap-Wearer, there's "the question of what it all meant—what was comic put-on, what desperate threat." As for the former, Ellison sees him "inviting all and sundry to admire and wonder in response to himself as his own sign and symbol, his own work of art." The man himself, Ellison notes—and the same, I believe, could be said for both men—"was hidden somewhere within, his complex identity concealed by his aesthetic gesturing. And his essence lay not in the somewhat comic clashing of styles, but in the mixture, the improvised form, the willful juxtaposition of modes." And for the viewer? the pitiable innocent bystanders, his "audience," if you will? Ellison claims that "whatever sheerly ethnic identity was communicated by his costume depended upon the observer's ability to see order in an apparent cultural chaos."

I love that: *cultural chaos*. Both men were using style—hair, hats, clothing, accessories; affect, attitude, and more—to heave a chair through the clear pane glass of American social presumptions. Ellison sees such gestures as a "freewheeling assault upon the traditional forms of the American aesthetic. Whatever the identity he presumed to project," Ellison insists, "he was exercising an American freedom and was a product of the melting pot and the conscious or unconscious comedy it brews. Culturally he was an American joker."

Like Ellison, I'm quite comfortable in an observational stance. I spend perhaps too much time cloaked, in the shadow, watching and witnessing and eavesdropping on the act. But what happens when the observer steps onto the stage? As interested as I was in Ellison's reading, his sense of what it all means, I was even more interested in these two men; I wondered what *I* might see when looking out through the eyes of the "American joker," the wielder of the "comic put-on," issuer of the "desperate threat." I had no idea what it would feel like to execute the gesture, rather than to "read" the executed gesture.

And to do so willingly, above all. I've acted in commercials and corporate videos in the past, but I never liked it, not for one single second, and I was always horrified and sickened whenever I was recognized in public—I'd frantically search for the "vanish" button, pressing hard, trying to disappear. I know what it's like to be a radio personality in a small town in the Deep South; being recognized always felt more like being under surveillance than being welcomed. I know the feeling of walking hallways in primary and secondary schools and having kids know your face, know your name, and you don't know theirs. If that was "popularity," I sprinted from it as soon as I realized the discomfort I'd feel.

This felt different. Both of Ellison's gentlemen seemed like pilots flying toward precise cultural coordinates, dropping bombs on cultural missions. Both seemed to have serious disruptive intent in mind as they toppled expectations and severed acceptable points of view. It's one thing to be a recognizable face, having done nothing other than managing to inhabit a hyper-visible space—it's another thing entirely to willingly fill up that space with conscious "aesthetic gesturing," with what Ellison calls a "clashing of styles," what he clearly sees as a "freewheeling assault upon the traditional forms of the American aesthetic." That's what I wanted to do, as moments passed, hair gradually grew, and I got that much closer to sprouting dreadlocks.

Death Sentence (i)

I delighted and reveled—and shook with stark terror—at the idea of stepping onstage, like my two worthy role models above. But I also wondered if I ran the risk of draining the antiestablishment value of dreadlocks by refusing, by being unable, really, to align the style with the familiar colorful clothing, the reds, blacks, greens, and golds, or distinctive "ethnic" olives, browns, and tans, the mudcloths and kente that so many dreads wear so well.

Ellison saw both of the black men he wrote about, a decade and a half apart on Riverside Drive, ultimately asking "the old abiding American questions: Who am I? What about me?" I wanted to exhume Ralph Ellison, I wanted to refill him with vivid, analytical life—and then feed him lunch—just so he could, one more time, long years after that second sighting, take his usual after-lunch stroll so that *I* could walk past him—in full dreadlock bloom. And what bothered me to no end was the possibility that he wouldn't find me sufficiently interesting to write about! That I wouldn't be the sort of stylistic oddity who would have caught his eye—that he'd just keep stepping, not even so much as bothering to stifle a yawn at present-day dreadlocks' cultural "impact."

Would dreadlocks still make a cultural statement if someone like me adopted the style? If I maintained a clothing aesthetic straight outta the suburbs, one that was relatively conventional yet put dreadlocks into the mix, would I diminish what dreadlocks are "supposed to" mean, in terms of black hair and the inherent rebelliousness of the style? I would hope that the "clashing of styles" would be of sufficient interest to provoke Mr. Ellison, but how could I be sure? Modern dreads were originally born by Rastafarians, and had gradually "grown" (shrunk?) into a style worn by American blacks, and a few whites, autonomous enough to wear them and still make a living. Would melding them to my Los Angeles suburban mentality and sartorial style further grow—or "shrink"—the style itself?

I didn't know. I wanted to know, I was eager to know, but I couldn't know. I was troubled by the prospect of damaging a style I had so much affection for, and even if I was bringing that old Marx Brothers joke to blazing, uncomfortable life (said Groucho: "I would never want to belong to any club that would have someone like me for a member"), I was determined to do it. I tried to assure myself that it would take thousands, if not millions of folks like me to smooth out the bumpy cultural impact of American dread. I didn't *really* think I could destroy it all by myself. But I knew that if it did happen, if dreadlocks became just another hairstyle—on my watch—that I'd never forgive myself.

Dreadlocks, My Favorite Hairstyle

Novels: Trey Ellis's *Platitudes* and John Barth's *The End of the Road*; films: *Harold and Maude* and *She's Gotta Have It*; music: Fishbone and Living Colour and the Wynton Marsalis Quartet.

I've been naming those favorites for years. I fell in love with Barth and *Harold and Maude* as an undergrad. And the go-go post-soul years of the mid-to-late 80s spawned *Live at Blues Alley*, Spike Lee's and Trey Ellis's first efforts, Fishbone, and Living Colour. I was young, I was impressionable, and, without fully realizing it, I was intent on scouring American culture for mirrors, for echoes. I was looking for myself.

For what else are "favorites," anyway? Declaring something "favorite" is far, far different than declaring something "best." Favorites are intimate. In order to become a favorite, a work of art must speak to something inside you—whether it's a whisper or a scream.

Favorites are us, really; they must be. Favorites are mirrors. We love who we are, and we are whom we love. We might like a work of art, we might respect it, appreciate it, admire it, but that alone won't allow it to ascend to Mount Favorite. We must see ourselves in it, as it, of it. I am *Platitudes*. I wasn't a chubby, romantic nerd at sixteen, but I am *so* Earle Tyner, the male protagonist in *Platitudes*. I am the withdrawn, socially awkward Harold, delighted to finally meet his Maude. I'm not insane, and my morals and ethics aren't nearly as squishy, but oh my God, I truly am Jacob Horner of *The End of the Road*. I was a ghost fifth attendee of Thanksgiving dinner in *She's Gotta Have It*; I was an invisible, onstage hand-clapper at *Blues Alley*; I stood next to Angelo and performed my own shadowy "scrotum check" on tour with Fishbone. I am the Cult of Personality.

And I am dread.

The hairstyle circled nonstop in the air above my head for years, patiently flying in a holding pattern as I matured, as I became ready and able to try and possess it, to earn it, to live up to it, to own it. And when it finally landed on top of my head, there was no question that it would become an affectionate favorite of mine, a favorite-among-favorites, a mirror of who I am. Because on some level we don't choose favorites—they are revealed to us. We might think we select favorites, but I don't think we do; we recognize them, because they're familiar, because they are us. I am dread.

Our bodies broadcast favorites, commonly known as "personal style." With hair, with clothes, with accessories, we wear our favorites for all to see, whether we consciously realize it or not. No stranger watching me on the street could possibly know my favorite novels, or music, or films—or even know I had favorite novels, music, or films. Those works of art might speak to me, but they don't speak for me, out in the world, like dreadlocks do. It's impossible for anyone watching a dreaded head to know who that dread is, even if the locks trigger cultural concerns inside the heads of watchers, allowing them to think they know. Cutting through all that social noise—to the watcher, to the wearer, to the world—is the assurance, by all, that with everything it takes to achieve them, dreadlocks must surely be a favorite hairstyle.

Dreadlocks: a public declaration of love.

Advertisements for Our Selves

Style, like personality, evolves as the individual changes and is an intimate response to one's time and place. Style is a dialogue between the individual and his world. True style demands courage and an ample dose of generosity and humor.

—Bill T. Jones, dancer and choreographer

This Bill T. Jones quotation spurred me to thinking about how I could develop a clothing signature, one that could emerge along with my slowly growing hair. I'd been going out into the world just any old way for far too long. Jeans, T-shirts, sneakers. I'd been doing that for years, and as 40 years old stared back at me from my mirror image, that style felt somewhat adolescent to me. I did want to go outside, but I also wanted to do it as a grown-up. Now, although I did wear all black occasionally, and though I certainly wouldn't have wanted to become one of those pretentious schmoes who wore black and only black every day, I did want to formulate a consistent fashion statement, one that I liked, one that I was comfortable with, one that was coherent, but also one that would speak to something intrinsically "me"—the adult me—and yet was fashionable at the same time, whatever that meant. I had a couple of buddies who consistently wore cowboy boots. Novelist Reginald McKnight has a fleet of vests—I can't recall ever seeing that brother divested. Hollywood TV producer Paris Barclay has, as of this writing, seventeen pairs of Hush Puppies. Tom Wolfe and his daily high-collar white shirts and white suits did come to mind.

Of course, the mixture of dreadlocks and fashion just made the idea all the more risky. Locks is a style, a hairstyle, but it's also something of a fashion accessory, a component of an overall look. Nobody walking around in clothes hasn't also done something with whatever is growing—or not growing—out of his or her head. Hair is the yin to clothing's yang; it's more than mere punctuation, but it's also less than definitive, since it doesn't stand alone. They're in cahoots—or they're shouting at each other—either friendly, or mortal enemies, or even frenemies, but they're always in some sort of conversation.

I had an idea of what I wanted, but the hazy relationship between head and clothing interested me far more than the actual head and the actual clothing. Where's the line, where's the boundary? I saw a white guy in a music store not long ago wearing short, conventional, freshly cut hair and a standard, off-the-rack-at-Target shirt-and-shorts combo. He would have been completely unremarkable except for his ear gages—the black-plastic, quarter-sized discs that his earlobes were stretched around. His ears were floating alone, bolded, italicized, and in a completely different font than the rest of his body's adornment. He might as well have had tiny mortar fire and mini rocket-propelled grenade launchers aimed at each other, a vicious firefight having broken out across his body—that's how much at war his lobes were with the rest of his attire. Not a good look. He was incoherent—and not pleasingly so. His ears were rebelling against his clothes. (I should say that he was, from across the store where I stood surreptitiously watching him, utterly conventional in his manner and his affect, as he seemed to shop for an electric guitar. No flamboyance, he.)

The problem is that it's all so frustratingly, gloriously, subjective! And so necessarily transitional. And who can tell, really, staring across a sparsely populated music store in suburban Richmond, where this guy is headed? Remember: I'm the buzz-cut brother who said, *I am dread*, even when he was still far, far away from hair growth that anyone could actually see. Who knows where this guy's going—or been? Might he have come from a barbershop earlier in the day, where the waist-length hair he once had is still waiting to be swept up off the floor? It's all possible; our bodies are temporal billboards; they're momentary Maileresque advertisements for ourselves, even if we don't know—can't know—exactly what the product is.

Hair Drama (i)

Dread consumed me, bite by mental bite. Chewed me up and swallowed me down. I was driving back home after dropping my daughter off at school one day, slowly snaking through downtown Worcester, when I turned left on Main Street toward Walnut Avenue and—whoa—I spotted a natty dread walking up the sidewalk! He had corralled his long, unruly dreads into a ponytail that reached to his lower back. He'd collected them, he'd tamed them—so that he could go to his. . .office?! (This was Main Street, after all.)

I backed off the accelerator and immediately began losing speed. Pretty soon my wheels were barely turning, my vision split as I tried to watch both him and the remaining rush-hour traffic. His attention was straight ahead as he walked purposefully, completely unaware that he was playing the starring role in an improvised theatrical street production I'd quickly titled *Hair Drama: The Case of the Corporate Dread.* As I spied on him from behind, I couldn't help feeling like some cheesy babe-hound who was surveilling an unsuspecting, voluptuous, ten-on-a-ten-scale woman. The difference is that Babe-Hound would have had to say something nasty or catch her eye, wink, lick his lips, and then blow a kiss—he'd have had to make sure Voluptuous Woman knew the Hound was checking her out. Me, I was simply curious; I remained covert.

Approaching gradually, I observed his oversized white shirt, his mustard-colored, slightly-too-large corduroy pants, and his well-worn loafers as he busted up the south sidewalk, striding toward Worcester's business district. I pushed down on the accelerator ever so slightly, easing forward. For a step or two it was as if we were, indeed, on a movie set: The camera panned right and picked up his profile, and—"roll tape"; "speed"; "*...action!*"—he wasn't a man striding down the street, he was a dolly-shot actor, his dreadlocks rippling down his back in gauzy slow motion as he stepped past the gleaming cars of a parking lot. I gradually pulled ahead, peeked right to look back at him, and...yes, sure enough, he was wearing a tie! *How 'bout that*, I thought. *Corporate dread. On Main Street, no less*. I have to say that was a first for me.

Actually, in one way, it didn't look all that strange. He was, after all, slightly disheveled; his somewhat rumpled clothing disrupted that "sharp" look most corporate boys are after. He wasn't wearing a jacket, and the baggy shirt and pants, if he was minus the tie, would have had him ready to hang out in the park, instead of ready to sit at a desk. But he was wearing a tie, and he did have a bag slung over his shoulder that fairly screamed "office" and proclaimed that he was headed to "work"—and it was coming up on nine o'clock, after all. His "aesthetic gesturing" wasn't quite as confusing as Ralph Ellison's sightings of Mr. and Mr. Cultural Chaos fifteen years apart on Riverside Drive in New York City, but I'm delighted to report that I wasn't at all certain what this brother—and his clothes and his hair—were trying to say.

But stalking Corporate Dread was nothing; it was a mere momentary eye in the twister of a spin I was in: I was blissfully, eagerly trapped in a whirling, howling dreadstorm. It was the exact opposite of a whiteout: When I looked around, all I could see was dread. Everywhere. I tried to pay attention to the Brian Blade Fellowship, for instance, when I went to see some jazz at Regattabar in Cambridge. But dread elbowed into the way, obstructing my view. At one point in the first set, bass player Chris Thomas sat down and played with his hair while Blade took an extended drum solo. I'd seen Thomas play maybe three times in various cities across the country over the previous few years, but this was the first time I'd ever seen him twisted. As Blade flailed at and pummeled his drum kit, Thomas calmly sat inches away, onstage, absently twisting his locks in exactly the way I imagined Omar twisted his own "wig of thumbs" in "Palm Wine," a Reginald McKnight short story. It occurred to me, as I watched him, that maybe the difference between his dense, micro-dreaded hair and more traditional long-form dreads was this: His dreadlocks hadn't "locked up"; they were still twists. He looked as if he could comb his twists out at any moment; right there onstage, he could pull out a pick and round his hair into a natural if he wanted to. That was his prerogative, of course, but then, that must be why they looked different than "real" dreadlocks, why they looked less legitimate to me. I recalled that Sam Perkins, when he played for the Seattle SuperSonics, wore something similar. It wasn't a permanent hairdo, it was more like a temporary style. Suddenly, as I watched, Thomas jammed his fingers into his hair and scratched, and you could see that there really weren't individual dreads, just a mass of hair with little dreadsticks sticking out.

Intentionality (ii)

The first written evidence of dreadlocks is in the Vedic scriptures, which are of Indian origin. The Vedic deity Shiva wore the style. The word used in the Vedic scriptures is "jaTaa," which means "wearing twisted locks of hair." In fact, several figures in *The Ramayana*, including mighty Rama himself, wear what sound like dreadlocks to me. *The Ramayana*, like the Vedic scriptures, were developed and written about 2,500 years ago, and the scriptures are the foundational texts of Hinduism, and influenced Buddhism and even the Celtic religion (the Romans said the Celts had "hair like snakes").

Both Egyptian royalty and commoners wore dreadlocks in ancient Egypt. The Egyptian dynasty began a little more than 5,000 years ago, and anthropologists have found mummies of ancient Egyptians with dreadlocks—the Egyptians wore dreadlock wigs, as well.

Germanic tribes, the Vikings, the Pacific Islanders, the Aztecs, early Christians, the Baye Fall of Senegal—the question isn't who has worn dreadlocks. A better question is, who *hasn't* worn dreadlocks at one time or another?

Original Dread (i)

Most Westerners today associate dreadlocks with Jamaica, and with good reason: Here in the West, anyway, the dreadlock phenomenon emerged from Jamaica, before it spread to Britain and to the United States.

But who invented dreadlocks in Jamaica? What was the spark that lit the fire? Was it the 1923 book *Ashanti*, by R.S. Rattray, which contains photos of images of the dreadlocked *Okomfo*—as well as the Akan people of Ghana? Or images of Ethiopian monks in *The Abyssinians*, by David Buxton? More than one version of how "matted locks" came to be associated with the Rastafari suggest that some clever, contemporary Rastas saw a depiction of Africans wearing dreadlocks in the Jamaican press. One account suggests that the pictures were Gallas, Somalis, or Masas—or that they were Jomo Kenyatta's freedom fighters, the latter a suggestion that there's a direct connection between Rastafarian dreadlocks and the warrior image of the Mau Mau. Yet another argument is that dreadlocks were inspired by Indian *saddhus*, religious mendicants whose presence in Jamaica was documented by a 1910 photograph. But then again, some insist that published photos of Haile Selassie's tribal guards—called the "Mountain Lions"—are the impetus for Rastafarian dreadlocks. Who really knows? The truth could be a combination of several of these theories or one of them or something else entirely.

It's impossible to tell. But we can tell who they're most associated with, who wore them in the West, and about whom the most mythology has emerged: the Rastafari, pure and simple. And we also know why they consciously "elected," as Barry Chevannes put it in his book *Rastafari: Roots and Ideology*, to wear dread, even if the intent of that process was nowhere near as organic and "natural" as I, at least, originally thought: They wanted to go outside; they wanted to be outsiders. They wanted to make a statement to Jamaica and the world that said, "against Babylon." "They elected to wear their hair matted, like the outcasts from society, because not only were they treated thus, but they did not consider themselves part of it," writes Chevannes. One thing's for sure, Chevannes concludes, and I couldn't help but smile knowingly as I read the words: "the innovation was intentionally symbolic."

Original Dread (ii)

A young prince named Tafari became "Ras," or king, of Ethiopia in 1927. He was known, therefore and thereafter, as Ras Tafari. After three years, he was crowned King of Kings and given the name Haile Selassie I. In December of 1932, a charismatic man named Leonard Howell recognized Ras Tafari as a living god and began to preach, began to spread that gospel, praising Ras Tafari in his home country of Jamaica. And no, Leonard Howell, dubbed the "First Rasta" by some, did not wear dreadlocks. He was, by most accounts, a dapper and well-groomed man. In fact, Rastafarians came to be known by their hair, but it wasn't hair growing on the top of their heads—it was hair growing on their *faces*. From the beginnings of the Rastafari on into the 1950s, Jamaican newspapers derisively called them "Beardmen," "Bearded Men," or, simply, "The Beards." It's up to historical question, actually, whether all of the early Rastas actually did have beards or if the preoccupation with their beards was a media creation or assumption. Haile Selassie I was wearing a thick, full beard when he appeared on the cover of *Time* magazine on November 3, 1930 (the first black person ever to grace *Time*'s cover, by the way). When Leonard Howell returned home to Jamaica and began to spread the word about Ras Tafari, it made sense that Ras Tafarians would wear beards, in honor of their deity. There were small numbers of followers at first, but early on nothing much was made of the beards they wore—until the wearing of beards began to become associated with the Rastafarians a decade or so later.

There were, along with Howell, three other leaders of this gradually developing Rastafarian movement. Each of these men had their own communities, or camps, and each had an autocratic, charismatic leadership style. Howell's community was called the Pinnacle (more on the others below), and since he supervised a wide-scale ganja farm—and spread his crop far and wide on the island of Jamaica—the close association between ganja and the Rastafari began there, and continued until the Pinnacle was destroyed by Jamaican authorities in 1954. This top-down, domineering leadership style adopted by the first generation of Rastafarian leaders certainly gave the second, younger generation something to rebel against. And while that rebellion also had to do with a variety of doctrinal stances the younger Rastas disagreed with, a large part of the disagreement had to do with hair, but still not the hair on their heads—the question was whether or not to wear beards.

Going Outside (iii)

I flew to Colorado Springs during the second week of March 1998 to present "'She got short, nappy har well as I': Black Hair and Social Hierarchy in William Wells Brown's *Clotel*" at a regional popular culture conference. Val was right: My hair looked awful. I was happy I didn't know anyone at the conference. Still, on the way to the hotel from the airport I peeked around corners and ran to the elevators like a fugitive, on the run from the B.H.P.D.—the Black Hair Police Department. I was almost embarrassed to leave my hotel room. I knew when I stopped cutting my hair it was going to look pretty rough for a pretty long while. I also knew that I would just have to get used to it. I just wish knowing all that would have made it easier. Finally, the next day, I swallowed whatever sense of decorum I once had and walked out of my room and toward the elevators, pressing the call button in order to head downstairs and give my paper. The mirrored walls of the elevator car tortured me all the way down to the floor of the room where I was to give the paper. Every way I turned on that elevator, no matter which angle I used, all I saw was hell up on my head. Finally I just closed my eyes, trying to make it all go away by plunging myself into willful darkness. Luckily, the elevator didn't stop; no one else got on. I longed for a Halloween mask, a paper bag, anything to hide the shameful torrent on top of my head.

• • •

As it turned out, my hair was the least of my problems. I had known full well that presenting a paper that interpreted a mid-nineteenth-century literary text at a popular culture conference was a risk, but I had no idea how risky it would turn out to be. As best I could determine after my panel's presentation, only one woman in the room had actually read Brown's novel. You could say that the reaction to my paper was not exactly stellar. Number of questions I got? Zero. Comments? Right about the same amount. But I was intrigued by that lone *Clotel*-reader. She was, not surprisingly, the only black scholar in the audience. She did walk up and give me some feedback as we stood in the lobby afterward, and I appreciated that, but her words were not the most interesting thing about her. She was fiftysomething, petite, wearing a tasteful, flecked-with-gray natural, sharp, tight specs, a gray flannel skirt suit, and a kente scarf around her neck.

Her attire, her hair, the collected signs of her public presentation were, I thought, talking loud *and* saying something. She was issuing unmistakable political commentary as she blurred sartorial boundaries. She was both corporate *and* anticorporate. Even though the kente and the hairstyle would not likely be found on a black woman in the corporate world, this woman wore a suit that looked exceedingly corporate. She had, by skillfully combining hairstyle and accessories, placed herself inside a tradition and yet tweaked and commented on—critiqued—that tradition at the very same time.

As I watched her snappily striding toward the hotel elevators after our conversation ended, I wondered if dreadlocks would do something similar for me. *I'm so tired of "safe," of "conservative,"* I thought. *I wanna go outside.* At the same time, I truly felt like I just wanted a different hairstyle, even if I was wary of the "just" that I had just used. I did know one thing: The hatred I felt for my messy hair was growing more passionate by the second. This interim term, this awful, ugly space of growth-time, was excruciating; I hated that I looked so much like a boob who needed a haircut, and quick.

• • •

As soon as I got back to Worcester, I dropped my bags and headed right back to the mirror. My hair looked utterly obscene. If it looked bad the day Val outed me, and if it was tortuous in Colorado, this day it looked like the scorched, burned-out residue from a forest fire. It was hair befitting the day it was: Friday the thirteenth of March. It was scary. I mean, I understood that my head was going to look wretched for a pretty good while. But I didn't think it would look this bad.

The main problem was that I had been cutting my own hair for such a long time. After being able to just pick up my clippers any time I wanted for so many years, this new fuzzy phase was going to take some getting used to. By the end of April, my hair had grown so much that it was tough to slick on the pomade and keep it tight and clean. Actually, it was impossible. I just gave up and combed it out instead of encouraging it to lie down neatly. I tried to pat it down into some sort of shape, but it didn't wear well at all.

I looked unkempt. The good news, of course, was that struggling to get it to look halfway decent did point to the rapid growth my hair has always had. When I was cutting my hair regularly, fast growth was a pain. Now that I wanted it to grow, fast growth was a pleasure. But as quickly as it was growing, it grew far too slowly for me. As I stood there, scowling at my Friday-the-Thirteenth hair, I wasn't entirely sure if I would ever truly get used to it. I did know that I had a long, difficult journey ahead of me, and if my hazy head was bothering me this much this soon, I had skinned my knees on the very first step.

Original Dread (iii)

In the 1940s, tension among the Rastafari was growing. Brother Watson, or Wato, was one of the fiery young men of the second generation; the Rastafarian camp he developed in the late 1940s grew into an organization called the Youth Black Faith. While there were other disagreements—on dogma, on ritualistic questions about the usage of candles, and more—the wearing of beards was a huge issue. Wato, in *Rastafari: Roots and Ideology*, complained about a Rasta named "Brother Downer" who

> used to lick out against a man who carry beard, for him don't carry beard—him shave clean. So in fi him House him never like fi see much of the beard man come in. Him call we ram goat. So it always fiery to I how you teaching about His Majesty Haile Selassie, and is a man who carry beard, yet among the brethren you just on the brethren about his beard.

At bottom, it was a classic tale of elder experience and caution against youthful aggression and rebellion. Leaders like Leonard Howell had to deal with the police—and had to deal with the way the police felt about the Rastafari. Whereas Howell struggled with police harassment in the course of his missionary activities, these Youth Black Faith members "seemed bent on inviting confrontation," as Chevannes put it. Whereas Howell and other leaders were not afraid to stage pitched combat with the enforcers of the law, the Youth Black Faith "were contemptuous of the law itself and seemed to delight in demonstrating it." This elder/youth tension inside the Rastafari played out on the bodies of the members of the faithful. No surprise there, since hairstyles and facial hair communicate to society who you are and how you see yourself. So the Youth Black Faith rebelled against any sort of visual "sign" that might make it seem as if they were compromising with the larger society. They wanted to wear beards, and would wear beards, and Brother Downer and whoever else be damned. The bearded young men of the Youth Black Faith grew in number, and influence, within the movement.

Part of the attraction for these young men was their sense of disciplined duty and fidelity to the Rastafari itself. "They used to say I was very 'dreadful,'" said Wato. "I was very strict to my duties to see that a man don't come anytime him want to come. Him come whenever the time is appointed. If we say the house is to meet tomorrow morning to discuss something, I always stand up to see that him don't come ten o'clock or twelve o'clock and all that time. I am always strict to them things." The deep religious conviction that these men felt collectively earned them names like "Warrior," and, yes, "Dreadful" or "Dread." And it was also the YBF that was responsible for the institutionalization of dreadlocks. From the beginning, for the YBF as well as the larger Rastafari community, there was a reluctance to cut hair, both on their faces and on their heads, stemming from the Nazarite vow in the Bible (Numbers 6:1–21). But that didn't mean that there was the same reluctance to *comb* that hair. The question of combing was the source of the tension.

Eventually, discussions about whether to comb or not, to lock or not, became so hot that by the mid-1950s the Youth Black Faith split into two factions: the "House of Dreadlocks" and—are you ready for this?—the "House of Combsomes."

It might seem, from safe historical distance, that the debate was somewhat trifling—I mean, who would guess that a *House of Combsomes*, of all things, could emerge from the Youth Black Faith, that a split could arise among something so seemingly trivial as hair?

But it wasn't trivial. It wasn't trivial at all.

I can completely understand the tension. And I wasn't the least bit surprised that the Dreadlocks won out, either. In embattled organizations, and sometimes in organizations not so embattled, but especially if they're made up of passionate young people, extremes often carry the day. It's a lot easier to stand on either pole and scream into the middle than to stand and hold the center. Surely the Dreadlocks felt that the Combsomes were being too conciliatory with their wish to comb, and that stance clashed with the "warrior" mentality of the Dreadlocks.

So the Dreadlocks used dreadlocks to create and sustain an identity, to express group solidarity, and to disturb and provoke society. All of this happened years before the hairstyle migrated to the United States. But even though we now know why second-generation Rastafarians wore dreadlocks, the question still remains: How did they decide to do so? There were derelicts in Jamaica, as there are just about anywhere, and like damaged people on the margins of society everywhere, some of those derelicts had matted hair—but where did the Dreadlocks get the idea to cultivate their dreadlocks? It might have been something as simple as the growth of beards and hair accidentally locking up—for reasons having directly to do with Rastafarianism and not combing. That's hard for me to believe, though.

• • •

The coincidence struck me. There I was, trying for all I was worth to grow out my hair, to commence dreadlocks as a way of signaling to the world my own difference, my own attempt to step as far outside of myself as possible while still *being* myself, and on some level the originators of the style, the vaunted Rastafari themselves, *also* adopted the style as a way to send a message—of difference!

Legend has it that the name "dreadlocks" emerged not much later. According to Hélène Lee's *The First Rasta*, a follower by the name of Jah Bones was sitting around with four other Rastas, and Bones "felt that the new hair style should get a name. A man suggested fear locks and immediately the other four say no. I think it was Danny," he recalls, "who said why not call it dreadlock since that sounds better, and according to the dictionary it means fear." Added Jah Bones, "That was in '59, closer to '60 than to '58." My face broke into a wide grin as I read those words and recognized my birth year right there on the page. I rocketed up out of my chair, tossed *First Rasta* aside, and fist-pumpingly declared my belief that this crucial naming conversation actually took place in April of 1959, precisely on the eighth day of that month. Hence, in my fertile imagination, the name "dreadlocks" and the body and mind of "Bert Ashe" were born on the exact same day.

Growth

Original Dread (iv)

The year I heard the word "reggae" for the first time was 1974. I was fifteen years old. Considering how I feel about dreadlocks, it's been a nagging source of guilt ever since, that I've never really liked reggae all that much. And since I could always take or leave reggae, it's odd that this episode would stand out in my memory. One day during that summer of 1974, I was with my folks at a get-together, visiting friends of the family in suburban South Pasadena. I'd just loaded my plate with seconds, and I distinctly recall overhearing my older sister excitedly talking to a couple of her friends over by the pool about this mysterious new word Stevie Wonder had used on *Fulfillingness' First Finale*, his new album. "*Boogie on/reggae woman*," Stevie's song went, and the question lingered in the smoggy summer air: What is this thing called…"reggae"?

"Raggay. *Rag*-gay," they whispered to each other, trying it lightly on their tongues, like some sort of taste test. "I wonder what it means," one of them said. "What *could* it mean?" said another. I'm sure I was on my way to another part of the house, ready to hang out with friends my own age, but I paused, because although I'd also heard and liked the song I, like them, had absolutely no idea what a "reggae woman" could be.

In some sense that teenaged, pop-culture info-gap reveals just how uncool we truly were, although I really should speak for myself. It's hard to tell just what cultural currency Bob Marley had in the US in 1974; it wasn't until 1976 and *Rastaman Vibration* that one of his albums showed up on the American pop charts. Even so, the Wailers had been around for ten years already, and while Marley was and is the biggest reggae artist ever, he wasn't the first one, nor, obviously, the only one. Something tells me we should have known—and would have known, if we were cooler, if we were closer to the outside. Stevie Wonder obviously knew what reggae was, even if his attempt to reproduce the actual sound of reggae on his hit record was an abysmal failure. If we lived closer, culturally, to where Stevie lived.... Still, my seventeen-year-old big sister and her suburban black friends had no clue, and neither did I.

I suppose the question can, then, be begged: If I had no clue as to what a "reggae woman" could do, how could I have known anything about reggae? Or Marley? Or—without question—dreadlocks, before the age of fifteen? I don't believe I did.

• • •

It didn't take long for me to find out more once I got to San Jose State, although I have to believe I'd heard of Marley sometime between hearing Stevie's song and the fall semester of my freshman year. But even if I hadn't, Yvonne, the rabid Marley fan across the hall, would have been delighted to introduce me. What was even more interesting was when Yvonne told me that her older brother had a reggae program somewhere on Bay Area radio, and that he had dreadlocks, to boot. Shortly after she got to campus, she placed a huge poster of Marley on her wall, his dreadlocks splayed in classic performance mode, and she often played his music—alternating with her beloved show tunes—at ear-splitting volume.

This is the way culture roams. This is the way informal knowledge spreads. A stray song here, a vivid poster there, a reference to a dreadlocked brother by a classmate. I never knew his name, and I'd prefer not to know his name—he'll always be "Yvonne's Dreadlocked Brother" to me. He didn't really exist for me as a human being, as such, as opposed to a tantalizing idea, this shadowy, unseen American black man out there, living and breathing under dreadlocks, spinning reggae for a public radio audience in the San Francisco Bay Area, a man whom I've still never seen, a man whose mere existence deeply fired my eighteen-year-old imagination and curiosity. Yvonne's brief, casual mention of her brother was likely my first introduction to the idea that someone who was not Jamaican, not Rastafarian, and not a reggae musician might actually wear the style.

That quick conversation, right there, is as close to an origin myth as I can recall, something along the lines of The Day I Realized Dreadlocks Were an Option for Me, Even If I Was Over Twenty Years from Exercising That Option. I wish I had recorded the actual date of my conversation with Yvonne, but I hadn't; I had no idea, on that day, that it was in any way a special day. (But then, I also wish I had moved, with gusto, toward actually locking my hair back then—but I didn't do that, either. I was so far away from "ready" to start the process that I didn't even know "ready" existed.) I couldn't know at the time how significant this slight, small exchange between across-the-hall dorm buddies would be, but I now know that by the time we parted and went our separate ways that day a tiny, disruptive dreadlock "cell" had unknowingly been planted in my imagination, and from that moment on dread-cells began slowly dividing and multiplying deep inside my mind—even if at the time I didn't consciously realize that it was happening.

Let's just say it took a while for that idea to take.

• • •

At bottom, I remain a disc jockey. I remain happy and proud that I pursued that career. Yes, I did eventually leave it, and I'm far happier to be a college professor today, but there are odd, unexpected parallels between the two professions. Putting together a text-after-text syllabus isn't too terribly different from putting together a song-after-song radio show. It's about the blend, even more than it is about the segue. I love breaking down the boundaries between each text, finding similarities and connections between them, pointing out the differences, particularly if they differ in similar ways. Context is key. A jazz radio show, like a course on jazz, lives inside contexts we both recognize and can't even see, contexts that emerge from the listening to and reading of recordings and novels and poems—and, in the course's case, in the midst of vivid classroom conversation. The selections, the texts, float around inside cultural contexts that I try to teach my students to recognize, so that a third of a way into a show—or a few weeks before midterm—the groove of the show (or the readings) should gradually become obvious. The best shows, the best courses, trap you, delightfully, in the groove. And I can *twist*; I can doggedly collect and turn a handful of locks into one fantastic super-lock until that lock becomes a sustained dreadlock of its own. I can become as comfortable as possible with my hair, but there will always be a familiar fuzziness above my hairline, a comforting disturbance, an irregular regularity trapped in the groove.

Barely Avoided Spit-Take

Before spring could turn to summer in 1998, Val and I and the kids rolled south from Worcester to Richmond for my doctoral graduation from William and Mary. Whenever we visited Richmond we'd stay at my sister-in-law Niecy's house, a snug two-bedroom ranch on a cul-de-sac in Chesterfield County, where she lived with her boyfriend, Keven. That time we arrived midafternoon, a few days before graduation, let ourselves in, and unpacked. By the time Niecy came home from her office, I was lounging on her couch, resting up, reading.

"When're you going to twist it up?" she said brightly, as soon as she walked through the door.

I dazedly looked up from the book, almost disoriented. I said, "Excuse me?" You'd think they were twins. Niecy's just as intuitive as Val is, I thought to myself. Maybe they're secretly empaths, like Counselor Troi and her mom on *Star Trek: The Next Generation*. Or maybe it's genetic, maybe they share some sort of extrasensory familial trait. My wife and her sister obviously shared something that allowed them to peer past my growing hair and into my dread future. Could it have been that obvious? You'd think that "Dread here, soon" was tattooed to both sides of my neck, an arrow pointing up at my hairline.

"You know, get twisted," she said. "When are you going to get twisted? What's the plan? I could twist it for you right now. Or I could show you how; you could do it yourself."

I just looked at her, as she blithely continued to put her keys and other items away. "Isn't it still too short?" I said finally. "I thought it needed to be longer than this."

"No way, man. You can easily twist what you've got."

"Really?" Finally, someone with knowledge. And I wanted to know it all. She flamed the teapot in the kitchen and then I followed her around the house, asking as many questions as I could think of. I badly wanted information about the process of dreading hair, on care and feeding, if nothing else. At the time, I felt as if I knew less than nothing. While imaginary dread-cells had, indeed, been growing inside my head since the late 1970s—and by this time, twenty years later, my imagination was flooded with dread-cells too numerous to ignore—the process somehow remained an abstraction to me. Dreadlocks seemed so natural to me that I simply didn't think about process much, especially since I was thinking so much about appearance.

At the same time, I have to say that there simply wasn't much information to be found on the cultivation and maintenance of the hairstyle. I had, of course, scoured the Internet as best I could in this pre-Google, pre-YouTube, pre-social media era—but there wasn't much out there to discover. So even though Niecy couldn't tell me as much as I wanted to know, she knew a lot more than I did. After settling in and pouring tea, she dropped the bomb.

"It takes two months to get dreads? *At least* two months? You're kidding." I was stunned. As I was to discover in the months to come, it actually takes longer than that. "Well, here's my plan," I said at the time. "I let it grow long, longer than it is now, right? Then I have Val braid my hair. After a few days I have her remove the braids. I get under the shower, wet the separated strands, and then let it dry without combing."

Niecy took a sip of tea. She started chuckling.

"Then I go a few days without combing. In fact, I'm thinking I'll never comb again after that shower."

Niecy was in full-blown laughter by now, having stopped sipping, apparently in order to avoid a vaudevillian spit-take.

"Eventually all the tubes of hair harden, and voila: I have dreadlocks."

In the end, Niecy's nonverbal reaction—prolonged, table-slapping laughter—suggested to me that "eventually" would be a long, long while.

It was a fairly informative conversation, helped along by the fact that Keven, a working musician, had worn dreadlocks for several years, and so Niecy had some close-at-hand knowledge. Mostly I learned that I had a lot to learn, but I also received some technical knowledge about maintenance—chiefly that there's far more of it than I realized. The big question, it seemed, was this: How do you keep the wannabe locks in place while they go about the process of locking up? According to Niecy, you had to continually twist them, keeping them separated until the locking process is complete. Apparently, it would, indeed, take a few months—at least.

There were some questions she couldn't answer. Like, what caused grouped strands of hair to "harden," anyway? What made the hair fuse together? Exactly what happens to the hair externally that causes it to seemingly alter its previous qualities? Or did it literally grow differently? And how is that possible, after all? If hair is supposed to be dead stuff once it leaves the body, then how does it "lock up"? How's that work?

I didn't know. Niecy didn't know, either. I did learn so much, though, that when Val asked me a few days later when I was going to stop combing my hair, I knew enough to tell her it wasn't quite that simple. At all.

What I realized from talking to Niecy, though, more than anything else, was that the process was much more maintenance-heavy than I'd first imagined. But I was still dead on target. *It's happening*, I thought to myself, *I'm determined. There's no turning back now.*

"Professorial." (i)

I did the South-West-North triangle in fourteen days. I went to Richmond and Williamsburg, Virginia, for my doctoral graduation; I feverishly prepped for and then made a mad dash to San Diego to present a paper at the American Literature Association conference; then I made a harried streak back across the country to Providence, making a breakneck blaze up Route 146 to Worcester in order to catch Game Seven of the NBA conference semifinals. By the time I reached home, I was exhausted.

Predictably, the graduation party, held at Winnie's Caribbean Cuisine in Richmond, was the place where I received the most intensive reactions to my increasingly lengthy hair. Most of the guests hadn't seen me for a year or two, and those who had seen me as recently as a few months before were still stunned at how long my hair was. Now that I think about it, if I had been a guest at my own graduation party I would have been shocked at myself. It's not that hair growth, in and of itself, is that unusual, of course. Let's face it: But for male-pattern baldness, hair emerges; that's its job. People cut their hair in order to style it to their preference, but hair does, indeed, grow. What else would it do?

But I had relentlessly cut my hair so close for so long that I guess friends and family had certain expectations. When, via their ears or neural impulse, "Bert Ashe" appeared in their brains, they'd open a file that contained all they knew and remembered about me, and apparently the visual space in that file had me in the close haircut I'd sported for so many years. Must have been, because folks were mighty surprised that I had altered that expected visual. I had just emerged from the rental car and was standing on the sidewalk outside Winnie's, ready to go inside, when one brother inquired about the length of my hair. I deadpanned something about how it was as short as ever just last week, and that it had grown this long virtually overnight. We stood there, silently staring at each other for several seconds, during which I swear I could see Belief, the challenger, in one corner, and in the opposing corner, the champion, Disbelief, leave their respective corners and move out onto the surface of this brother's face, instantly mixing it up. When I finally grinned, effectively declaring Disbelief the rightful victor, he looked kind of hurt, as if I had made a fool of him. And I suppose I had, although that wasn't my intention.

To most of the inquiries, I replied that the length was a symbolic gesture to mark the occasion of my receiving my PhD. "You know the way some players—or teams—will shave their heads before a big game?" I said a few times. "Well, this is roughly equivalent—but I couldn't shave my head because that would have been too close to what I'd always done. So I went in the opposite direction."

• • •

As it turned out, it wasn't so much the length of my hair that everyone found so peculiar, although in Richmond it certainly was that as well. No, what was odd—and completely unexpected—was that people in Worcester and in Richmond and in San Diego, people who'd known me for the space of a conference weekend (scholars I met for the first time in San Diego), people who'd known me for a couple of years (Holy

Cross colleagues), people who'd known me for a few more years than that (William and Mary professors), and people who'd known me for long years (professors from Virginia Commonwealth University, where I got my master's), even people who'd known me all my life (my sister)—all had their eyes affixed to the *gray at my temples* more than anything else. And what almost all of them said, in one way or another, was that it was "distinguished" and, sometimes in the next breath, that it was "professorial."

"Professorial." *Professorial.* I remember reading an article in the *Chronicle of Higher Education* a few years before about a new female professor who had difficulty fitting into what she considered to be an appropriately "professorial" image. She tried on the tweed jacket, for instance, and also the accompanying Imperial Presence persona (best exemplified by John Houseman's magisterial Professor Kingsfield from *The Paper Chase*), and they simply didn't fit her. (Didn't work for me, either; I'm closer to a genial talk show host than Professor Kingsfield.) But the focus of the article was that painful space of time in between her attempt to fit what she thought was a preordained role, and her eventual realization that she would have to alter her sense of what "professorial" meant for her. She finally found her own conception of what it meant to be a professor, how she could credibly *perform* the *role* of "professor."

I never had that problem. I mean, sure, I certainly had my adjustments to make when I was hired at Holy Cross, but performing the role of professor simply was not one of them. After I left radio and television, I spent a few years managing the evening callers who executed surveys at a market research firm, before heading back to school. That experience had given me a credible jazz "head" off which I could riff and solo in the academy. I knew what I would wear, what my in-class demeanor would be, what my syllabus and classroom policies would be. Still, I suppose the crucial question is this: How much did my immediate success in the role of professor have to do with the (external) expectations of my colleagues and students combined with my own (internal) comfort zone? The two must have blended, there must have been a profitable admixture, or else I would have struggled as well. The business pages used to say of Bill Gates things like, "He may be the richest man in the world and run Microsoft, but he looks like an accountant!" The Richmond *Times-Dispatch* sports pages often used to refer to Terry Holland as "professorial" while he was head basketball coach at the University of Virginia. Americans definitely have a mental image of the way people who work in certain occupations should look. (The nerdy, smart-assed computer guy; the rigid, terse LAPD Aryan cop.) Holland often wore a tweed coat, he was 50 or so years of age, he was gray, he was white, he was male. Presto: He was "professorial." And somehow, gray hair at my temples had folks seeing me as "professorial" in a way that, it seemed, more than a year of *actually being a professor* apparently did not! I include "it seems" in that last sentence because if I'd arrived at Holy Cross with "distinguished" gray at my temples, I suppose people would have already thought I looked "professorial" instead of saying I *now* did after a change in my appearance, and—what—would never have mentioned it otherwise? Hard to tell.

It may seem inconsequential, this "professorial" business, and on one level it was; I'm absolutely certain that the astonishing number of friends, family, and strangers who mentioned it barely gave it a first thought, let alone a second. But the aggregate surely speaks to a cultural assumption that explains why that young female professor felt fitting into it was so important. If she doesn't fit, I remember her writing, then *is* she a professor, really and truly, inside and out? Tough question. I say, "Yes. Absolutely. As long as you have, or can gradually develop, your own conception of what the 'performance' of 'professor' means to you."

And anyway, I was far more interested in what the world meant by "professorial," what that image sustained in their heads, than my having had to struggle to match that image. My response to the Gray Question was, most of the time, "Well, yeah, but you're only seeing the gray now because I let it grow. I'm telling you, it was there all the time; it was just cut short." It was in the midst of a conversation with novelist Paule Marshall, as a result of her complimenting me on how distinguished and professorial I looked as we sat at adjacent tables at Winnie's during the graduation celebration, that I realized—and I shared it with her when it occurred to me—that it's possible the gray *wasn't* there all along, that I *was* more gray than I used to be, that even though it was cut short, my long hair could very well have been revealing a relatively recent growth of gray. It reminded me of that *Seinfeld* episode in which Elaine Benes dated a guy who had been shaving his head completely bald for some years. She was curious, so she asked him, "What do you look like with hair?" She eventually nagged and teased him into trying to grow it back—and he couldn't. During the space of time he'd been shaving it, he'd been slowly going bald—and never knew it. He was appalled, to little surprise. (Predictably, Elaine, for her part, quickly lost interest in him.) Similarly, although my hair was, for years, too short for me to be aware of it, I do think my temples *were* slowly graying. It only told on me when I let it grow. Whatever, there it was: I presented to one and all my "distinguished," "professorial" graying temples!

What made it all so secretly amusing was that I knew this is just a way station, a pit stop, a brief layover before I got twisted. So virtually every time someone said something about me looking "professorial," I would conspiratorially chuckle to myself, thinking, *Enjoy this look now, my friend—because pretty soon I'm going to shed this skin, too.* Before my parents left town we went back to Winnie's for dinner. Just before the waitress brought our food, a dreadlocked man walked in and headed to the back. My mother, a snicker at the back of her throat, nodded at him and said, "You going to have something like that?" I looked at him quietly for a moment or two, then softly said, "Could be…"

Dread Lit Syllabus (i)

"As much money as you've got, you still can't comb your hair to see your mama."

My father stood in the kitchen and instantly crowded the room. Just an inch shorter than I am and sixty-five next month, he's still thick and immovable wherever he stands.

"Hi, Papa. I've told you. They're dreadlocks. You can't comb them out."

"If I were a roach or a water bug, I'd look at that rat's nest of yours and think I'd died and gone to heaven. Come on over here, boy, I've got a hacksaw in the garage."

He pushed my head down in the vise of his bent arm and pantomimed sawing off my locks. Everyone laughed, including Avon and Allison, who'd appeared in the back door. Avon, my big brother, who is forty-five years old and now as thick as he is tall. Allison is forty. She must have just ironed her hair because the room suddenly smelled of distant toast.

"Papa, you say that every time you see me."

"And I'll keep saying it till you chop off them little monkey dicks."

"Virgil!"

"Well, that's what they look like. You've said so yourself."

"I never did no such thing! I think they look just fine, baby, if that's what you want sitting on top of your head."

—Trey Ellis, *Right Here, Right Now*, 1999

Art, Science, Religion (ii)

Black hair, how—why—do I love thee? Walk seven pathways to my heart…

I love black hair…

because it can be "read" three related ways: the aesthetic, the political, and the interpersonal. Those three tenets, those three cultural lenses provide black hair with the cultural "pop" it has and has always had. All three exist on a level, interpretive plane, each no more important than the other.

I love black hair…

because it's intimate. In most cases, teach a nonblack little girl to brush her hair and I'm thinking she can do it herself from the age of—what—four? five? younger than that? slightly older? From then on she gradually absorbs her cultural and gendered understanding of what "beauty" means—to the world, to herself—at the beauty parlor and in her daily life. Little black girls get the weekly beauty parlor vibe, *plus* they're sitting between moms, pops, or some caregiver's legs on the daily, facing away, likely on the floor, as her head gets hooked up. And quite often that's a time for sharing, for interpersonal intimacy—and, yes, perhaps a time for screaming through tender-headed fire—but it's always a time for physical closeness.

One of the many ways that Spike Lee's *She's Gotta Have It* was magical and transformative for me was that simple scene when Nola Darling greased Mars Blackmon's scalp. I immediately recalled walking down the hallway in Moulder Hall at San Jose State and peering into dorm rooms where similar rituals were being enacted—girl sitting on edge of bed, guy sitting opposite on floor—over and over, day after day after day. And the way Nola complained about Mars's dandruff? The way she lightly and affectionately rapped him on the head with the comb when she was finished, like end punctuation? That's it right there, that's the sustained, beautiful intimacy black hair confers. Always. Somewhere in America, somewhere in the world. Right now.

I love black hair...

because it's political. But it's not narrowly political; too many black people don't realize that. Black hair is an unreliable narrator. Sometimes critical viewers forget about play, about fashion trends; they forget that one of the important things about wearing a style is that others are also wearing that style. But black hair is, indeed, political, meaning the wearing of a particular hairstyle is an implicit—sometimes explicit—political act. The easy example is the way the Afro was worn by 60s militants to accompany their revolutionary demands, as well as the Afro grown to annoy the hell out of parents and the rest of society. White countercultural boomers did the same thing with the length of their hair.

Sometimes the act of wearing black hair is intentionally political, sometimes it isn't, but how a viewer reacts to a hairstyle is sometimes politically motivated as well. Not once, in any of the black churches I've belonged to as an adult, have I ever been invited to be an usher. Val believes it's because of my hair. She believes that the uniformity that black ushers in black churches nearly always display (wearing the same color suits, often the same color ties and pocket squares, walking uniformly down the center aisle to receive and then distribute collection plates, that sort of thing) would be disrupted by my dreadlocks, which is so unlike the sharp, clean haircuts of the other men. I'm not so sure. I always felt it had more to do with me never giving off even the slightest interest in being an usher, and the man who's in charge of ushers either consciously or unconsciously picking up on that distinct lack of interest. She might well be right, or I might be right. Both of us might be right—or neither. Either way, the issue is politically inspired, one way or the other; there simply is an implicit political dimension to the wearing of black hair, a dimension that can become explicit at any time, springing up suddenly to surround the most unsuspecting wearer, such as an innocent, braids-wearing young woman told by management she can't wear that style at work, or a black child attending a private school who is well liked, even beloved—until the kid shows up one fall with dreadlocks and is summarily dismissed from campus.

I love black hair...

because it's a means of personal, artistic expression. Valerie always had Jordan hooked up with beautifully designed braids, swooping circular lines that gracefully blended into angles to create the sort of hair that was persistently being complimented. Yes, Val sat down with her daughter's head of hair beneath her hands, but she just as easily could be seen as an artist sitting down to create; it's just that it's Jordan's head instead of a canvas, Jordan's hair instead of paint. This is the sort of aesthetic expression that's been going on for thousands of years, since long before the new world. Hair shows are great ways to see black hair as art. Or just hang out in urban areas and keep your eyes open.

Now, none of this is unique to black hair. Around the time I got twisted, I taught a class called "Hair, Hoops, and Jazz: Explorations in African-American Expressive Culture." And the same interpretive pathway I used to understand black hair I also used to get a toehold on jazz and basketball. Jazz is political—many buckets of ink have been spilled over the years talking about what Charlie Parker and the bop movement meant, for one, and what the free jazz movement of the 60s meant, for another. And those are just the specifically politicized years;

the act of getting onstage and placing a saxophone or trumpet in your mouth and blowing, or grabbing sticks and stroking skins, is an inherently political act. Jazz music is, of course, artistic expression, and the bandstand is a nexus of interpersonal communication, with band members musically talking to each other and the band musically talking to the audience and the music they're playing responding to the call of previous jazz eras as they simultaneously send a call out to future jazz musicians. Aesthetic, political, interpersonal.

I love black hair...

because it demands choices, explicitly. Perhaps more than any other sport, basketball requires that its players—essentially two jazz quintets playing with a ball and hoops instead of instruments—also play with and against each other, with and against the opposing team, and with and against tradition. Disruptive black style, as expressed by forceful, improvisational basketball intent, has long been seen as commentary on how basketball "should" be played—which makes that intent political, whether the players mean it to be or not. That style itself, elevating physical movement to the level of art, filled with pump fakes, stutter steps, asymmetrical misdirection, bursts of speed, sudden stops, hang time, throw-downs, and trash talk, is absolutely a means of self-expression. And, yes, on-court and beside-the-court interaction between players and waiting-to-players does, indeed, create a site for interpersonal exchange, and possibly intimacy.

But you don't have to play basketball or pay any attention to it at all. You don't have to like jazz or pay any attention to it at all. You don't have to attend a black church, or listen to hip-hop, or play the dozens; a black child adopted by white parents who live in the wilds of Maine with only other white people around, whose cultural rituals are not at all associated with performed blackness, still has to deal with black hair. Black hair demands choices—you have to "do" something with it. It is insistent. It is belligerent. It's *in your face* even if it's *on your head.* It refuses to be ignored.

I love that.

I love black hair…
because you really can't pull the three strands apart; they're locked together. The aesthetic? The political? The interpersonal? I separate the three to talk about them, but in truth, they meld, like individual lock-strands on a multi-month fusion-quest. When Val braided Jordan's hair, the result was a free-floating signifier, an artistic text created by Val, expressed by Jordan. The contours of Jordan's head provided the rough terrain that Val had to work with, something like the surfaces found in nature some artists prefer to paint on. Even hair as express-political-statement has an unmistakable aesthetic dimension to it. Even if there's no explicit political statement involved, the existing aesthetic dimension was almost invariably created through some form of an interpersonal relationship. Black hair is collaborative, it's interactive. It just is.

Do these three aspects of black hair have nonblack hair referents? Of course. Do other races deal with some of these same issues *as much*? Kinda. Sorta. Surely, there's a political referent; go watch the movie *Hair*. Other than the political, though, I don't see direct comparisons that truly work. It's the kinky, truculent roughness of black hair that I love, the aggressiveness of it. Asian hair doesn't seem as demanding. Nor European hair—black hair laughs at that whole Marcia Brady, brush-a-hundred-strokes-a-night-to-make-it-shine business.

I love black hair…
because it's a window on the soul of black America. Long—or short—may it grow…

"—or short—"

By midsummer, 1998, I was speeding back to Worcester, Val beside me in the car, both of us having moments ago stepped from a Me'Shell NdegéOcello performance at the Iron Horse in Northampton, Massachusetts. Absolutely fantastic show. She was funky, she was funny, she played some old favorites, she played some new favorites. And yet, as we stomped and head-bobbed and fist-pumped and applauded our way through the show, all I could think about was the soft whisper of hair upon her head. I didn't know it at the time, but she had recently cut off her dreadlocks. Her hair was cut about as close to bald as possible—about as short as mine was before I let it grow. And so it seemed curious to me that as soon as Valerie and I walked into the venue, one of the first things I noticed was how many young black women in attendance had the exact same cut Me'Shell was sporting. Now, the Northampton area has a heavy lesbian presence, and NdegéOcello is bisexual, herself, and so I couldn't help wondering if the black women who were wearing the closely cropped hairstyle were also queer. And then I thought of Cheryl Dunye, the writer/director of *The Watermelon Woman*, who is black, and lesbian, and wears her hair cut close to the scalp. I shared my observations with Val on the hour-long drive back to Worcester.

"So what does it all mean?" I asked, expansively. "*Is* it a hairstyle for black lesbians?" I raised my index finger, professorially. "Actually, more importantly, even if it is, should it be recognized as such?"

"What are you talking about?" Val said, grouchily. "Why don't you just ask some black lesbians?" She had recently taken a job as a research analyst for a Worcester area HMO; she had come straight from her office and we had gone directly to the show. She'd had a great time, but by now she was a little tired, and perhaps more than a little tired of me.

"I mean, think of it this way: If a group gets together and adopts a certain style, then it seems to me that adopting that style says something about that group's identity. On some level, it's a way of identifying with each other, as well as a way to express that identification to the world, right? Something like gang colors or even sports team apparel. Crip says, 'Yo, I'm a Crip; I wear blue so my crew knows what's up—and so Bloods know, too.' Raider Fan says, 'I'm a Raider man; I wear the silver and black so suck-ass Dallas Cowboy punks know what's real.' Both groups wear what they wear so they'll recognize each other, and so the rest of the world will know who they are, too. See what I mean?"

Val sighed. She looked out the window.

I kept talking. "What if an extremely short haircut is a way of saying, 'I'm a black lesbian; I like the style, but I also wear my hair short so other black lesbians will know who I am.' And that—"

"Bert, here's the problem: I'm pretty sure there are black women wearing their hair that short who are straight. And I'll bet there are plenty of black lesbians who wear their hair longer. What about all of them?"

"I hear you. Yeah. And you'd probably win that bet, too. But see, that's what makes the possibility of close-cropped female hair as black lesbian sign so interesting: Do enough people know about it? Most people in LA know that red means Blood and blue means Crip—sometimes your very life depends on knowing that. And really, the Raiders and Dallas Cowboys are national corporations masking as sports teams; even people who aren't football fans know about them. But a buzz cut on a black woman? How many people—outside of the gay community—know immediately what that could mean?"

"But maybe it doesn't so much mean 'black lesbian,'" Valerie said, "as much as, say, 'progressive, nontraditional black woman,' you know? A woman who just wants to look different. Isn't that possible?"

We said it together: "…kind of like dreadlocks."

I left her alone; we drove the rest of the way in silence. But inside my head, the question remained: If that close cut was, indeed, a Black Lesbian Hairdo™, would they want it to be recognized as such by those outside the community? I'm not sure. I would think so. I do think it would be fabulous, though, whether the greater public had knowledge of it or not, if there was a specific lesbian hair aesthetic, so that if one black lesbian saw another one that she didn't know who was wearing that hairstyle she could step to her and whisper secret lesbian code words in her ear, and if the right words were whispered back, they could do the secret handshake and there'd be a connection forged, based largely on a hairstyle. The style would literally identify, from one woman to another, the possibility that they were a part of the same "people" based on some more or less identifiable physical sign. Made sense to me.

Going Outside (iv)

So much of men's fashion is centered on the neck. Western male fashion codes evolved over several hundred years, and the area surrounding the neck seems to be the nerve center for one's clothes. The simple task of reaching up to a collar (a collar with a tie looped through it, encased by a suit coat) and unbuttoning that collar, loosening that tie, takes one or two seconds, tops. But that simple gesture is the difference between being appropriately formally dressed and being "relaxed" and informal. Heaven forbid someone actually *not* wear a tie to an event—a business meeting, a dinner, church—that would seem to demand one. It's the neck. I think a lot of people focus on whether there's a tie or not, but it's really the closing on the neck that truly matters. That's the stylistic boundary: "dressed" on one side, "casual" on the other. The neck is the battleground; "winner" or "loser" is up to the wearer—and the observer.

• • •

I've always admired nonconformists. Admired them from a distance. In my early years, I was not only a conformist, I was a hyper-conformist. Conformity, after all, is just a form of willing invisibility, a way to blend in, to exist and yet remain unseen. If I was truly a nonconformist, I'd've had dreadlocks back in the 1970s, when true fashion rebels, like Yvonne's brother, began adopting the style. And yet, as I waited for my hair to grow long enough to twist, I knew I didn't want someone who could watch me from across a music store to be too lazily content, either, in thinking they'd "gotten" me. I want to needle that watcher. I want to be provocative. But I also want to be comfortable in my own skin, too. And I wanted to have both, simultaneously. I wanted a look that was not only comfortably "me," but also one that was both "consistent" and "chaotic," if, indeed, that's even possible.

Actually, I already had a consistent fashion statement. I blended in with millions and millions of Americans: jeans and tees for casual wear, and a button-down shirt for "dressy-casual," with Nikes or loafers. But I wanted more than that. I was starting with my hair, but the other four-fifths of my body needed attention, too. "People make choices about their appearance for all sorts of complicated reasons," writes Robin Givhan of the *Washington Post*. "And often, they glom on to a cliché because they find it reassuring and easy. They wear the dress of a particular social tribe because they want people to make assumptions about who they are—because letting folks come to a conclusion on their own is often easier than having to explain." That's all too true, I'm sure, but I was struggling to find a way to avoid dread clichés, as well as trying to disrupt the "reassuring and easy" way people might see me once I grew locks. I didn't know exactly how to do it, but I did know that's what I wanted to do. As long as I could somehow remain myself—as long as I could be as close to comfortable as possible.

After all, Bill T. had it right: Style *is* an evolution "as the individual changes"; style *is* "a dialogue between the individual and his world." And since I'd only be changing so much, I thought I'd better develop a clothing aesthetic that riffs on what I was wearing at the time. I thought I'd keep some of what I had already, and mesh the clothing that I could see myself "evolving" into, as well.

Tied Up/Tied Down (i)

I am not a different person with a tie than without one, even though some people's perceptions of me will change with my clothes. Even my fellow passengers, reluctant as they are to take the seat next to mine, probably look at me a little bit differently than they would were I in my jeans…

—Stephen L. Carter, "The Black Table, the Empty Seat, and the Tie"

Here was my thinking at the time: If I abandon an aesthetic that I must like, since I'm wearing it, I wouldn't be executing a Jonesian "evolution," I wouldn't be having a "dialogue" between me, between *who I am*, and the world. I'd be executing an obliteration, a fraudulent renunciation of who I am. Now, the hair might be deemed a revolution, since it's so totally different from where I started. But the clothes are absolutely an *evolution*, like Bill T. Jones says. And not only that, but as Jones insists, "True style demands courage and an ample dose of generosity and humor." So: As of March 1998, when I first hatched this hair-brained scheme to grow dreadlocks, I was often wearing a Levi's shirt (or a blue "work shirt" or an olive green camper shirt) and occasionally a nondescript tie with my Levi's jeans and old-as-dirt brown shoes. I was thinking that I would keep the Levi's jeans as my suburban-roots, who-I-am base, but mesh that with a striking, colorful, natural-fibers shirt, one that would be unusual and clever, with a dashing, striking tie. And what if I employed a fleet of cool shoes to wear with my Levi's, as well? I'd squash the sneaker-wear and only wear shoes.

And here was the kicker: I wanted to wear this new style *always*. At the time, I only wore ties in class. When I was on campus and but not scheduled for class, I'd often dress "casual," meaning a T-shirt instead of a shirt with a collar. Well, I wanted to wear this new ensemble *all the time*. To movies, to hang out with friends, to campus on non-class days, to the office on weekends, to ball games; literally: always. I knew that when I first did it, people would probably say something like, "Wow, you're wearing a tie," at least, if the occasion normally didn't call for it. I planned to respond by saying, "Yup, I am. I like ties," and then move on to another topic. Soon enough, I thought, people would get used to seeing me in jeans, a cool shirt, and hip tie, and it would be seen, quite rightly, as my own style.

About Bob Marley...

Style mattered to Bob Marley. It had to. It feels uncomfortable to say so. I know full well how the American populace feels about style, the love-hate relationship it has with style. Anyone who pays too much attention to fashion and style seems frivolous, is seen as a person who doesn't quite understand that these things are irrelevant, that they simply don't matter, that what truly matters is what's inside. Anyone who discusses fashion and style must be facile and superficial, unable to move past the surface, and is to be informed of such at one's earliest convenience. I regularly read Robin Givhan's astonishing commentary in the *Washington Post*. She's a Pulitzer Prize–winning reporter whose beat is American style-and that's style as distinct from fashion, although she often talks about fashion, as well. Garments are objects to be worn; but which clothes are worn, and when, and how they're worn, has to do with personal style, and Givhan excels at exploring the broader American cultural meanings of stylistic decisions. And yet the consistently outraged online comments on her articles are shocking, mostly because they rarely engage what she actually says. Most commenters write in to insist that her cultural commentary about American style is a disgraceful waste of digital space. Style, commenter after commenter insists, is absolutely meaningless. It simply doesn't matter, they scream and rant and pout. It's remarkable, this consistently petulant, cranky response from Givhan's readers.

That's why I love Jonathan Lethem's tight, revealing response, the last sentence of his novel *You Don't Love Me Yet*: "You can't be deep without a surface." It's true. And yet it seems the overwhelming majority of Americans believe that style doesn't matter—even as they dress for certain occasions, even as the culture of celebrity is stronger than ever, and style has so much to do with who sustains celebrity and who doesn't. Style does matter. It doesn't matter more than our interior selves, but I don't believe it matters any less, either. There is a visual dimension to who we are. Our clothes, the way we wear our clothes, our bearing, our affect; the way we sit and stand, our voices, the words we use, the cadence of our words, eye contact—our style, collectively, communicates many, many things about us, and whether we want this to be the case or not is the true irrelevancy: Style matters; it always has, and it always will.

• • •

It almost seems like a waste of ink to write that from Bob Marley's head emerged the world's most famous and influential dreadlocks. They seem so fundamental to his being, so foundational to the way he performed his body, let alone his music, that it's as if he'd always worn them; was born with them; was a little boy playing soccer with them; wore them all the way through adolescence and his youth; and grew into a man beneath them. Bob Marley and his always-already dreadlocks were, it would seem, inseparable. I certainly thought so.

But Bob Marley had his own journey, just like everyone who locks his or her hair. The decision to lock, let alone the length of the process, insists on a journey. You can walk into a barbershop with hair down your back and walk out sometime later with a baldie; you can lay back in a beauty-shop chair and when you straighten back up you can have a perm; a dye job—or a conk job—can take place in a twinkle compared to the process of locking hair. Locking takes time—insists upon it—and therefore an interior journey of some sort will match the external locking process. There's too much time and uncertainty involved for that not to be the case.

Bob Marley's dreadlock journey is far more fascinating than I expected, and, not surprisingly, it was locked to, was tightly twisted around, the Rastafari. Robert Nesta Marley was born in 1945. He must have been aware of the Rastafari growing up; they were firmly established well before he was born. Whether he shared, as a child, the typical Jamaican revulsion for Rastas is unclear. Cindy Breakspeare, the mother of his youngest child, gives a sense of just how most Jamaicans in Kingston felt about the Rastafari: "We were not aware of it as a religious movement," she says in Christopher John Farley's *Before the Legend: The Rise of Bob Marley*. "I used to walk home from school every day from the back gate of Immaculate [Conception High School in Kingston], and if you saw a Rasta on the street, you would keep your head straight and hope that he didn't say anything to you. Because they were all crazy—they smoked ganja and they basically were all crazy. That kind of was the thinking at that time."

"In Jamaica, being Rastafarian, you were looked down upon, it wasn't like you were welcome anywhere," says Cedella Marley, Bob's daughter. "We were shunned by a lot of people. I remember having friends and wanting to invite them over to the house and they'd have to lie to their parents that they were going to spend a weekend at this other friend's house because the parent would never have them stay at my house." Cedella is describing Jamaica in the 1970s; Rastas were even less accepted between 1945 and 1960, Bob Marley's formative years.

Marley's growing interest in the Rastafari intensified around 1966, and according to Stephen Davis, in *Bob Marley*, mother and son went round and round on religion: "She was born and raised a fundamentalist Christian, and she didn't want to know about Haile Selassie. She was a member in good standing of the United Church of the Lord Jesus Christ of the Apostolic Faith, and here was her firstborn sitting at her kitchen table in Delaware, letting his hair grow into little knots and talking to her about Ethiopia." *This* was the Marley narrative I expected, neat, tidy, and propulsive: exposed to Rasta, intrigued by Rasta, becomes Rasta, locks his hair, grows into an international icon for reggae, Rasta, and Jamaica, dies a tragic death by cancer at age 36. End of story.

Reality is not so tidy. In the wake of Haile Selassie's historic visit to Jamaica in April of 1966, writes Davis, "Rastafarian consciousness had exploded," and Marley surely saw the effects of that expanded consciousness on his wife and bandmates when he returned from Delaware in October of that same year. Assuming Rita Marley, Bunny Wailer, and Peter Tosh uninterruptedly locked their hair after the events of 1966, their dreadlocks must have been pretty far along by 1973—but Marley's hair grew in another direction. Davis affectionately, almost lovingly, relates Marley's hair chronicles of the 60s and 70s: *1966*: "His hair, uncut during his last months at [his mother] Cedella's house in Wilmington, began to knot up and a sparse beard sprouted." *1967*: "Bob Marley was a farmer again…wearing blue denim bib overalls most of the time, his hair getting longer and knottier (though he kept it pent up in a wool cap much of the time)." *1968*: "Perhaps reflecting [a] new spirit of general rebellion among the young, especially among young black radicals, Bob Marley cut off his locks and combed out his hair in the fashionable 'Afro' style." *1970*: "Just before he left for England, on his mother's advice, Bob had his hair cut." *1971*: "Although Bob was not wearing Rasta dreadlocks at that point, he spent much of his time telling students about Haile Selassie and the repatriation of blacks to Africa." *1972*: "Bob appeared on tour wearing tight pants and an Afro hairstyle and sang like James Brown." And, finally, *1973*:

> [T]he Wailers packed their instruments, sweaters and overcoats and took off for London and their first tour. On the way, Bob went to Delaware to see his mother. Although Bob had worn his hair in modified dreadlocks twice before, he had worn an Afro style for the past three years. So when he got to Delaware, Cedella was surprised to see Bob's hair pent up in a red, green and gold tam, the colors of the flag of Ethiopia. At the kitchen table, Bob smiled and said, "Momma, look at this." He pulled off his tam and a new crown of sprouting locks popped out, kinky as kinky can be.
>
> "You growing it again?" Cedella asked, still dubious.
>
> "Yes, Momma."
>
> "Nes', you locksing up forever now?"
>
> "Yes, Momma."
>
> Bob Marley never cut his hair again.

Well. One thing's for sure: Bob Marley had, and will always have, The Most Famous Head of Dreadlocks Ever. But who knew he took such a circuitous road to the title? Who would imagine that a biographer would use the words "modified dreadlocks" in association with Bob "Icon-of-Dreadlocks" Marley? Now, Bob Marley was human, after all; I understand that, and I suppose that's the bottom line. But floating somewhere above that bottom line is the idea that Marley consciously or unconsciously associated his hair with his times, and linked that hairstyle with what was going on around him in the world, every bit as much as when he finally associated his hair with his Rastafarian beliefs.

• • •

So: There's Bob Marley in Wilmington in 1966, in knock-down, drag-out, kitchen-table conflict with his mother about how he wears his hair, incipient locks growing ever more dread as he speaks…and yet he doesn't finally lock his hair until *seven years later*? Those seven years could be read as indecision, as Marley wanting to lock, deciding not to lock, not yet, anyway, going 'fro, twisting, cutting, locking, unlocking—waiting for the right time, much the way I and many, many others did (although, of course, my locks never actually got started in the 1970s—or the 1980s—or most of the 1990s, for that matter). I see those seven years as an affirmative exploration, as a part of his long-locks journey into dread, as a way to marry his hair to his religious and political beliefs. Seven years: The space, perhaps, of time it took for someone who didn't want to disappoint and upset his mother; the time it took to finally assert ultimate control over his own hair.

I had no idea. I naively assumed he'd found Rasta, got locked, and his hair grew. So many people pinpoint Bob Marley as being their dread inspiration. Alice Walker, for instance, spoke for more than just herself when she said, "Bob Marley is the person who taught me to trust the universe enough to respect my hair." But I can't help but find it intriguing—refreshing, really—to discover that Bob Marley, of all people, would consciously "go Afro" in the late 1960s as did millions of young blacks in the West, as a way to symbolically declare allegiance to the black power movement. I love the fact that Bob Marley—Bob Marley!—took various detours to dread, moving forward, sideways, back, then renewing his focus and getting locked for good. We can't know for sure, but I have to believe that sometime in 1973, after years of indecision, he woke up one day, looked deeply into his bathroom mirror, and firmly and finally said, "I'm growing dreadlocks."

Tied Up/Tied Down (ii)

I wasn't sure how this tie thing was going to work out. Part of my attraction to the tie was nostalgic. I loved flipping through photos of dapper black activists in the 1950s and 1960s. (Malcolm *and* Martin, natch; they might not have agreed on much, but one thing they certainly agreed upon was looking good in dark suits.) Or movie stars of the era, or even people like Antônio Carlos Jobim cooling it on a boardwalk in Rio. The *style* they had back then! Suits and ties that actually fit, and fit to within an inch of their lives. Men did everything in suits, too—it was everyday wear that moved effortlessly, inside which they could easily do anything they might want to do. Sean Connery's James Bond, Bill Cosby in *I Spy*—these guys could run, jump, and fight wearing a nasty suit, and when finished, smooth down ties, head to casinos, and order drinks.

Oh, I'll admit it: I had a romantic attachment to that dangling, essentially useless piece of fabric. Slacks cover the legs and genitals. Shirts cover the upper torso, as does the suit coat, which also ventilates or warms the body. Socks and shoes have their function, as well. The tie? Superfluous. It hangs there, like a flapping cloth tongue, like a silk phallus—a huge, fat finger pointing down directly at the real thing mere inches lower.

Could I help rehabilitate the tie? Could I make it my own personal fashion signature?

Cousins

Summer arrived. The family reunion loomed. My head was so nappy I couldn't keep my hands out of it. I've always been fairly tactile. Little balls of hair that used to be restricted to the kitchen, to the base of my skull, grew ambitious. They expanded into chapters and regional affiliations, and then started holding nap conventions that seemed to include all areas within the circumference of my hairline. In terms of the way it looked, it was frustratingly haphazard; in terms of the way it felt, it was irresistibly attractive: I was always in my hair. I just couldn't seem to leave it alone. Val gave me a hard time about it, and I couldn't blame her. I looked terrible. I was just so tired of fighting with it. One day I jammed a cap on my head when I went for pizza, and Val stood by the door and shook her head in disgust. "So instead of combing your hair you just put a hat on?" she asked.

All I could do was nod grimly as I closed the door.

• • •

Los Angeles, California

Hair Drama (ii)

God knows there was massive hair drama at the Smith Family Reunion. At least, that's what I saw through the black-hair, interpretive-lens goggles now blowtorched to my face. My mother's family originally hails from Jeanerette, Louisiana. Since then, we've split into three additional locations: Texas City, Texas; Houston, Texas; and Los Angeles, California. This family reunion featured two distant cousins of mine, brownskin girls straight out of Louisiana who looked to be around fifteen years old. One had braids flowing straight down the middle of her back; the other had similar braids knotted on top of her head, with the rest of the length of it coming down her back, as well. These girls were wearing, and I mean *wearing*, long, braided extensions. Now, contrary to popular opinion, just because some blacks have hairstyles that seem to mimic white hair (straightened hair, conks, permanents, maybe even the Jheri curl), in no way does that mean they are "trying to be white." Kobena Mercer, in his seminal essay "Black Hair/Style Politics," put the smackdown on such silliness when he argued that black people who adopt such styles, whether they know it or not, are merely practicing a form of Western creolization. Mercer sees them as guilty of nothing more than cultural "play"—and I agree with him. (Lisa Jones said it best: Mercer's essay "puts the hair police out of a job.") My cousins were wearing braids, after all, a hairstyle that has been worn in Africa since before time began. So the fact that these girls (whom I'd never seen before) were wearing braids that flowed well past their shoulders could, in relation to Mercer's argument, be seen as moving far closer to Africanness than whiteness. Except for one thing: rampant hair-flipping.

Jill Nelson was interviewed on National Public Radio around that time. I heard her say that white women need to mute that hair-flipping business, because it's causing serious resentment from black women. I don't know how true that is, but the comment did send me straight to her book, *Straight, No Chaser*: "Aside from a brief period in the late 1950s and 60s when the 'Afro' was in style, the natural texture of most black women's hair remains, as it has historically been, unacceptable," writes Nelson. "The apparently never-ending popularity of a variety of straightening devices, from the hot comb to chemical straighteners—now euphemistically called 'relaxers,' as if the problem is that sister's hair is uptight and all we need to do is to get it to cool out—attests to this." Then Nelson seemed to square her shoulders and throw down for the home folks: "The proliferation in the last decade of hair weaves and braided extensions is a manifestation of black women's desire for hair that is not only straight but long, the better to toss."

After I read that last sentence, I wondered if Nelson had somehow seen into the future, as if she had visualized our Smith Family Reunion banquet in the Ramada Plaza Hotel ballroom. My two young cousins sang an absurd, elongated version of "His Eye Is on the Sparrow," complete with all the odd phrasing and overwrought bending and uncontrolled twisting of notes that so many young singers use and abuse nowadays. While I admired their courage and effort, it was how they punctuated the song that furrowed my curious brow. They finished, and as their extended family beamed and applauded, these two girls were careful to "carelessly" flip their long braids away from their forehead to behind their ears; with elbows high, they augmented the move with eyes-closed-little-shakes-of-the-head and stutter steps. They did it again and again, repeatedly tossing their hair, milking the applause. It was wild. There was absolutely no way these two girls could have mimicked such classic whitegirl beauty moves with such dead-on fidelity unless they had done much in depth, intense study, consciously or not.

Since the banquet was on Friday night, I watched them closely for the rest of the weekend. They weren't hard to find. Not only do we have a relatively small family, but they were always together, always showing off their legs, and always, always, always finding ways to perform their hair. My favorite moment came as we were leaving the California African American Museum as part of a black-oriented tour of LA. Just after they cleared the revolving doors, both of them, almost simultaneously, dipped their heads way forward, bending deeply at the waist, and then quickly jerked their heads backward, causing their hair to spill forward and then whip to the rear. I swallowed hard. It was a spectacular move. Kobena smiles; Jill Nelson frowns; Bert's just fascinated, regardless.

I really was curious about these girls, and they didn't even know I existed. Still, I wanted to talk, at least chat. So I gave it one good, solid, three-point shot. We were at the picnic the next day, silently tramping down what seemed like several thousand steps. I had gone with a group of younger family members to see a panoramic view of the Los Angeles basin atop a massive hill at Kenneth Hahn Park. Of course the two girls were together—they were always together. So I turned to the one next to me, and said clearly, in a purely conversational tone, "Is it true that you two are wearing some sort of device such that if you get more than ten feet apart you'll both explode?"

Now, I say things like that to young people all the time. Depending on their personality or what they think of me or a combination of the two, the response I get ranges from a smirk, a pleasant laugh, or good-natured exasperation, if I'm lucky, to a genuinely irritated roll of the eyes or a get-me-outta-here groan if I'm not. You know what I got from this girl?

"No."

That's it. All of it. Total. Voice: flat. Affect: zero. "No."

It was a roadblock no, actually, now that I think about it. It was not a no that said, "I hate you" or "Don't talk to me," because you have to care a little something to offer that sort of no. This was a dismissive no, an indifferent no, the Berlin Wall of nos, one that said, *You don't matter enough for me to use more than* even one syllable*; you should feel lucky I deign to use* even two letters *responding to your foolish query. So. Here's what you get, the most—and least—I'll give*: "No." I got the message, and we trooped down the rest of the steps in silence. But one thing I know for certain: Those girls sure knew what to do with their hair.

Twisted

Nature vs. "Nature" (i)

And yet there is something arresting about the episode: the writer sitting in his green retreat dutifully attaching words to natural facts, trying to tap the subterranean flow of thought and feeling and then, suddenly, the startling shriek of the train whistle bearing in upon him, forcing him to acknowledge the existence of a reality alien to the pastoral dream. What begins as a conventional tribute to the pleasures of withdrawal from the world—a simple pleasure fantasy—is transformed by the interruption of the machine into a far more complex state of mind.

—Leo Marx, *The Machine in the Garden: Technology and the Pastoral Ideal in America*, 1964

B.J. was late. I was bored.

The hair place was not just Twist and Shout, after all. It was Twist and Shout *Global Village*. B.J. was the proprietor. The shop took up a vast corner of a squat building in downtown Long Beach. Tracks laid on the adjacent street carry light-rail riders all the way to downtown LA. Inside the shop, behind a large plate glass window, in between a line of chairs for those waiting their turn, was a small, recycled-water fountain surrounded by plants and rocks, the system itself an island of manufactured nature in the midst of commerce.

I sat in one of those chairs. And sat. I had plenty of time to ponder the symbolic significance of the nearby railroad tracks (even if they were laid through an urban garden) and the body of water (even if it was artificially constructed). I had all the time in the world to spin these symbols around my own personal sense of dread exploration, the stylistic rebirth that would grow out of getting, at long last, my hair twisted into starter dreadlocks. I had all this time because B.J. was *a full hour late for my appointment.* There were a couple of employees on hand, either behind the counter across from the pool, serving fruity soft drink concoctions, or selling hair-care products behind another counter in another area of the shop. I was sitting by the fountain, bored stupid. I had browsed the table of books to exhaustion. I had drained my peachy drink. I had scrutinized all there was to scrutinize in the room. And so I sat, waiting. And waiting. And waiting—fighting, all along, to remain in good spirits.

"Hawthorne is satisfied to set down unadorned sense impressions," writes Marx, "and especially sounds—sounds made by birds, squirrels, insects, and moving leaves." It's calm there, in Sleepy Hollow. Quiet enough to hear such small sounds. "He hears the village clock strike, a cowbell tinkle, and mowers whetting their scythes." I sat, likewise, listening to soft reggae music, to water trickling through the pool, to quiet conversation across the room, when B.J., an example of human locomotion if there ever was one, arrived like, well, a noisy machine in a garden. She entered talking, pointing, bearing food, wrapping her smock, tiny, thin dreadlocks nearly horizontal as she whipped her head in one direction or another, moving here and there about the room before following her head to me: "Hello, I'm B.J., pleased to meet you. I'm sorry I was delayed," she said, briefly meeting my eyes before her eyes began critically interrogating my hair from crown to kitchen, left ear to right ear, and back again to repeat. Twist and Shout became a Global Village indeed when B.J. came back to the shop.

I was wary. An hour is an hour, after all, but she did apologize, and I couldn't resist what I can only call her vivid, pulsating life force, her *ashé*. And anyway, I didn't want to be downcast on that day of all days.

A Constructed Style that Appears Completely Natural and Yet Is Anything But

Can a hairstyle be postmodern? Is that possible? In the classroom, as a kind of shotgun introduction to postmodernism, I like to talk about the relationship Americans had with reality in 1950 and compare it to the relationship they had with reality in the year 2000. Bald, everyday assumptions made by the average American had flipped over completely during those 50 years. Objective truth just wasn't something Americans were repeatedly forced to question in 1950. A kind of what-you-see-is-what-you-get mentality held sway. But by the end of the twentieth century, and on into the twenty-first, our relationship with reality, with the very idea of objective truth, became far more complicated. The gap between perception and reality is wider than ever. In *1950*: A female, human breast was widely and anatomically presumed to be a natural breast, appearing on female chests as a result of pure genetics-in-action. In *2000*: A noteworthy breast might be surgically enhanced. Breasts enter a viewer's field of vision, and a 1950s observer simply wouldn't question whether or not those breasts have twin bulbs of silicone resting securely inside them.

In *1950*: Looking at a photo or listening to a recording, one could be reasonably certain that what the camera snapped or the recorder recorded accurately reflected the moment of capture. In *2000*: Viewers were all too aware that the untrained eye simply cannot tell whether a photo has been doctored; we know people or objects can be airbrushed into or out of photos, and we know we can't always tell. Listeners know that present-day sound recordings can make someone appear to say things they didn't actually say. In *1950*: If a major league baseball player hit a home run, it was unquestioned. Cheers if it was for the home team, groans if it wasn't.

In *2000*: Huge questions loomed as to how legitimate a home run was in the age of steroids and other chemical enhancements. In *1950*: One person talked to another person in one of two ways: face-to-face or on the phone. Other than that, the masses communicated by letter writing. The "media" were television, radio, and newspapers. Stores were brick-and-mortar spaces that one expected to walk into and out of. In *2000*: The internet and smartphones completely revolutionized human communication: there's e-mail, instant messaging, texting, chat rooms, gaming collectives, and more. The notion of cyberspace as a more or less actual "place"—as opposed to brick-and-mortar—and the myriad ways one can (mis)represent themselves online—was absolutely unimaginable for ordinary citizens in 1950.

It wasn't so much that indeterminacy—the question of objective reality—wasn't an issue in 1950 or 1850 or at any other time in human history. Representing reality in narrative form was always a problem. But in 1950, ordinary Americans didn't know it was a problem. We do now.

I don't think it's a complete coincidence that the dreadlock hairstyle emerged in an era when the perception of objective reality was as shaky as it is now (and forever after will be). Even before Madam C. J. Walker popularized chemical hair relaxers early in the twentieth century as a way to straighten black hair, there have been endless improvisations and variations on two ways to approach black hair styling: straightened or not. Even if a woman didn't "perm" her hair, she could "hot-comb" it into straightness. Men could "conk" their hair, James Brown–style.

The alternative was to wear your hair "natural," meaning to wear it in a way that welcomed and incorporated the kinky-coarseness of black hair into the style itself. This often involved cutting and shaping the hair, including rounding the hair, and sharpening edges at the hairline. In other words, in the mid-twentieth century, black hair had the same set of expectations Americans had about objective reality: black hair was to be styled, shaped, and/or cut in a way that conformed to the shape of the head beneath it. Even the revolutionary, militant introduction of the Afro in the 1960s merely extended the natural versus straightening black hair choice, though it dramatically raised the number of blacks who chose the natural side. Afros, however "natural," still needed daily combing, needed to be patted into place, because the look was a specific "look"—no matter that it was called a "natural"—and if the daily grooming wasn't done, the Afro just wouldn't look right.

Dreadlocks? Of course it's "natural," and, yes, of course, it's a "style"—and it must actively be styled, too, no doubt. Even most of those with tangled, messy, "roots"-style locks began by vigorously twisting, thus insistently encouraging the hair to grow in a certain way. But when it comes to looking at the style as observed when walking around in the world, one of the most striking things about this hairstyle is its seeming lack of definition: it's not "cut" into place, and it often appears not to be expertly styled in a way that is obvious (even if it actually is expertly styled). Any changes one might want to make to the style, any alterations to individual locks, take months, sometimes years, as hair slowly, daily melds with two or more twisted strands to form a larger lock.

Surely, some dreadlock-wearers, the most outré of the outré, shave the sides of their heads, turning their dreads into "dread-hawks," Fishbone-style. But those sorts of vernacular improvisations on the dreadlock theme have always been a part of black style, hairstyle or no. Dreadlocks are a living, breathing example of black postmodernism: ill-defined, appearing uncut and vaguely styled, yet fundamentally a constructed style, one that appears completely natural and yet is anything but. I don't buy that dreadlocks could have become widely adopted at any other time in Western history. Think about it: Dreadlocks need no chemical assistance. So there's simply no reason why the style *couldn't* have become an African-American phenomenon far, far earlier than it did.

I believe it took two things for dreadlocks to occur as a recognizable Western style. One, it took the expansion and decentralization of hairstyles for black males. By the 1980s, black males employed more popular, viable hairstyles at one time than ever before: the baldie, the buzz cut or Caesar, the fade (and its cousin, the high-top fade, or its second cousin, the diagonal "half"-fro), braids, the short natural, the resurgent Afro, the Jheri curl, and cornrows—plus the growing eagerness of many black males to cut shapes and designs into their hair. All those options made the introduction of dreadlocks, on some level, just one more soaring, improvisational riff off of a free-form hairstyle chorus—after a fairly two-note twentieth century of black hair.

But the other thing was that consciously or unconsciously, postmodernity encouraged certain style-forward blacks to value the lack of cut, shaped, and daily-styled definition on their heads. So much of the world's reality had gradually grown indeterminate; obviously reality existed, but it was increasingly squishy, spongy, and ill-defined. So what better time to introduce a hairstyle that, itself, was squishy, spongy, and ill-defined? It was black America's readiness, based on the West's growing postmodern reality, which finally ended in some of us actually welcoming The Dreadlock.

Twisted

The hairdressing chairs were behind a wall on the far side of the shop, cut off from the greater Global Village. Just as I was sitting down in B.J.'s chair, I heard a woman say, "That's going to look good."

I'd never seen this woman before in my life. Her hair was wet, and she was wearing a protective smock; she was a patron. She had wandered over to offer that fusion of compliment and encouragement, apparently because it seemed to her the thing to do. For me, it measured the difference between barbershops and beauty parlors. (Although this hair place was no ordinary black beauty parlor, that's for sure: no one was getting her hair fried, dyed, and laid to the side.) It had been a while since I'd spent time in a hair joint, barbershop or otherwise. I'd been cutting my own hair for more than ten years. Before that I went to a barbershop in Richmond's Shockoe Bottom, one in which there was zero chance one brother would say to another, "That's going to look good." Ritualistic insult was far more likely. ("Forget about your hair, son—where'd you get that *head* from?! That ain't no forehead, it's a *five*head!" And just as the laughter began to die down, somebody'd say something like, "Oughta call that nigger *headquarters*," to ignite the laughs all over again.) Storytelling, too. And spirited discussions about topics that merited a spirited discussion, mixed in with spirited discussions about all sorts of things that really didn't merit discussion at all.

"Glad you think so," I replied to the woman, smiling as she continued to gaze curiously at my head, as if she expected it to change form right before her eyes. It occurred to me that it soon would, at that.

Another woman was in the third chair, waiting for B.J. to give her a shampoo and retwist. (The process, it seemed, was even more elongated and difficult than Niecy made it sound.) Soon enough B.J. squared off and addressed my head. She agreed with the first woman: "Yes, this is going to look good."

Then she took me around the corner to get my head shampooed. Now, I've seen plenty of television commercials and movie scenes in which women are getting shampoos. Almost always the women wear nearly ecstatic looks on their faces—but I still wasn't prepared for just how pleasurable it would be. It didn't feel so terribly different from when I would shampoo my own hair, but everything else surrounding that feeling was wildly surprising: I could hear and feel the water on my head, trickling past my ears. It felt peculiar, ticklish and lush at the same time. I felt as if I was being fully immersed, even though I was fully clothed. I closed my eyes, which only heightened the sensations: the unexpected introduction of the cool shampoo, B.J.'s exploratory fingers massaging my scalp in one direction or another—I didn't know which sensation I would feel next—a rinse? more shampoo? more kneading?—and I didn't care. I surrendered all.

B.J. tapped my shoulder, and I rose. After wrapping my head in a towel, she led me back to her chair. Then she placed a plastic cap on my head and disappeared. (I was glad I couldn't see what I looked like; I'm sure I would have looked as ridiculous as I felt.) I was completely at ease, however, and I sat and chatted about books and authors with the two women in their seats. (Both of them were sorry they couldn't make that Friday's Toni Morrison reading.) B.J. returned and worked on one woman and then the other. After about twenty minutes, she removed my cap and asked me what thickness I wanted my dreadlocks to be. "About the thickness of my little finger," I said, showing her. "Something like that." B.J.'s dreadlocks were tiny, and I wanted mine a little fatter.

"So. Let me get this straight," B.J. declared. Her voice, though pleasant-sounding enough, could surely cut straight through marble. "I'm going to give you a dry twist, and then you're leaving? Going back to where?" B.J. was unhappy that I'd be leaving LA in a few days to go back to Massachusetts. She was bothered that she wouldn't be able to take me all the way through what she was calling "the locking process." Before I left, she gave me the name and address of a place in Washington, DC, that she knew shared her locking philosophy. I told her about a place in Worcester called Roots 'n Locks I had in mind for maintenance, but B.J. was dismissive; she was certain that they'd want to use chemicals. That was definitely not part of B.J.'s locking philosophy.

"Bert, you do not want to let those people put chemicals in your hair. That nasty, waxy stuff." She sharply sucked air through her teeth in disgust. "Sometimes they even put lemon juice in there." She was very explicit about just how disgusting my hair would turn out if I allowed that. "It's a shortcut, and it's not necessary," she insisted. "It's just not natural."

Then she started twisting. Before long, she didn't seem as concerned about maintenance. "Something in your hair just seems to *grab*," she said, with something in her voice that sounded like wonder. Beginning at my back hairline and advancing toward my forehead, she took small portions of my hair and gathered it in a long, fine-toothed comb, and then twirled the comb, and when she stopped and pulled the comb away, the "twist" remained. Then she went on to the next small portion of hair.

It took about an hour and a half. She's from Michigan, and we talked about that. I weighed in on living in New England, among other things. Finally, I steered the conversation to what I was really thinking about: black hair. She had a lot on her mind. For one thing, when the Bible says that Jesus's hair was "like wool"? She believes he had dreadlocks. I left that one alone. Maybe He did, maybe He didn't, but there's no sure way to tell, one way or the other. Then, maybe because so many people kept coming up and telling me how good my hair looked, I asked her whether black folks' historical notions of good and bad hair are completely flipped upside-down when it comes to dreadlocks. In other words, while people usually take "nappy" to mean "bad," and "straight" to mean "good," didn't, oddly enough, in this instance, "nappy" mean "good"? Another example where dread indeterminacy undermined social expectation?

She smiled. "Yes, in this case, 'good hair' is 'bad hair' and 'bad hair' is 'good hair.' But it's all good hair to me," she said. "I don't use those terms, and when people in my chair use them I have to straighten them out." I believed her.

Most importantly, I finally received an answer to the one question that usually got me shrugs or an "I don't know": Why—how?—does black hair lock up? "After all," I said, as B.J.'s hands continued to comb and twist, comb and twist, "the hair is out of our heads, right? So how does it happen? *Why* does it happen?"

She said that dreadlocks would naturally occur if we didn't do anything to our hair. "This hairstyle is truly 'natural,'" she said, speaking the words literally in the same instant she twisted yet another section of my hair, apparently completely unaware of the irony of her statement. She spoke to the "why" of dreadlocks this way: "African hair grows in circles."

If she said something next, I never heard it. I had already begun free-associating: I was thinking of Frederick Douglass and his "within the circle" description of African-American culture in his 1845 *Narrative*; I was thinking of the black vernacular tradition and the way black folk practice "group creation," implying an unending circle of call-and-response; I was thinking of prayer circle; I was thinking of the ring shout; I was thinking, as well, of specific black "circles": Harlem Globetrotters at center court, twirling to "Sweet Georgia Brown," the round of solos in a jazz quintet, even the unending rotation of the *Soul Train* line—God, what an amazing metaphor for the black vernacular! Even our *hair* grows in circles!

It all made sense then. Physically, dreadlocks happen because the hair grows in circles: Each solitary lock of hair creates an interdependent relationship by circling around other solo locks of hair to create a group, a large, freestanding strand, a "lock," which stands with other strands in order to become, finally, a head full of dread. Metaphorically, dreadlocks are a way of visualizing the blended mixture of black strands of difference and reality. And over time the circular process of combining and mixing these cultural strands, running through and over and under and around each other, produces a chaotic yet coherent black whole: the dreadlock. In that sense, then, I was wearing a prime metaphor for the rich diversity of blackness with every thin thread of hair that rotated up and out of my head. It "grows in circles." Of course!

Nature vs. "Nature" (ii)

But now, hold on: In a sense, this hairdo is no more "natural" than the 1960s Afro. Let's face it: It's a *style*. Around that time, I was reading Albert Murray's *The Hero and the Blues*. He put it this way:

> What makes a blues idiom musician is not the ability to express RAW emotion with primitive directness, as is so often implied, but rather the mastery of elements of esthetics peculiar to U.S. Negro music. Blues musicians do not derive directly from the personal, social, and political circumstances of their lives as black people in the United States.

In exactly the same way people who decide they want dreadlocks come to that realization, at least in part, by having seen them on someone else's head, blues musicians "derive most directly from styles of other musicians who play the blues," writes Murray. "In art both agony and ecstasy are matters of stylization."

As is black hair, if you ask me. Even the most "roots"-looking dread is participating in a specific "style." The fact is, that which would look "natural" is consciously *styled* to look "natural." "Not even the most spontaneous-seeming folk expression is artless," writes Murray. "Folk airs, ditties, tunes and ballads are labeled traditional precisely because they conform to well-established even if unwritten principles of composition and formal structure peculiar to a given genre or idiom which, after all, is an esthetic *system* in every essential or functional meaning of the phrase." The "system" was in place, then, when B.J. pointed to her own hair and asked if I wanted it like *this*, and I answered, relying on my *own* knowledge of the prevailing dreadlock "esthetic system," "No, I want it like *that*." Anything truly "natural," in other words, couldn't be so carefully planned—chemicals or no chemicals.

There is, in other words, a meticulously tuned machine in the garden. And why not? After all, who wants "natural"? If I had, I'd've just stopped combing and washing my hair and let whatever happened happen (although, of course, even if I consciously just let it grow "naturally," in order to achieve a specific *style*, it still wouldn't be truly "natural"). And anyway, why would I come to a hair *stylist* if I didn't want my hair styled? I did. And was it ever! B.J. finished her dry twist shortly after she finished her lecture; she awarded me an instructional brochure, made a follow-up appointment for Saturday, and sent me on my way.

Dread Lit Syllabus (ii)

The texture of her hair was somehow both firm and soft, springy, with the clean, fresh scent of almonds. It was a warm black, and sunlight was caught in each kink and crinkle, so that up close there was a lot of purple and blue. I could feel how, miraculously, each lock wove itself into a flat or rounded pattern shortly after it left her scalp—a machine could not have done it with more precision—so that the "matting" I had assumed was characteristic of dreadlocks could be more accurately described as "knitting." How many black people had any idea that, left pretty much to itself, our hair would do this, I wondered. Not very many, I was sure. I had certainly been among the uninformed. It was a moment so satisfying, when I felt my faith in my desire to be natural was so well deserved, that it is not an exaggeration to say I was, in a way, made happy forever.

—Alice Walker, *Anything We Love Can Be Saved: A Writer's Activism*, 1997

Veteran Responses/Rookie Responses

It's difficult to buckle your seat belt when you're at zero gravity. I gave up and rode home from that first session at Twist and Shout bumping up against the roof of my car like the Red Balloon. By the time I reached home I was absolutely, totally, completely smitten. I was floating like that cartoon dog does when he smells that scent he likes, you know? The one where he's lifted into the air as he goes, "Uh. *Unnh*. UHHHHH!" and then he comes floating down, sighing a contented "Ah-hhhhhhhh." Well, just leave out the "comes floating down" part, and that was me. I knew I'd have to deal with DC and that heavy what-to-wear question, but that was in the future. In August, in Los Angeles, immediately post-twist, I was very much in heaven. I thought it looked wonderful.

As I was turning into the Palo del Amo Woods subdivision, I discovered my father, mother, and my two kids were turning out. It wasn't until I reached home that I realized that I didn't have a house key. Luckily, they'd doubled back and let me in.

My father pulled into the driveway, turned off the engine, and gave me the keys. I unlocked the house and then returned to stand next to the car. My parents had an expression on their faces I'd seen many, many times throughout my life. It was the same expression they wore when I broke my nose, the victim of a mis-timed football double-reverse; or the time a dog I was petting bit clear through the webbing of my right ear; or when I told them I was dropping out of college halfway through my senior year to move to rural Louisiana to become a disc jockey. They're veterans, you might say. They know me. They're beyond surprise. But Jordan and Garnet quietly stared at me from their seats in the car, their mouths slightly open.

When she regained the power of speech, Jordan said, "You look like Mr. Keven," referring to Niecy's dreaded boyfriend. "It looks like a bunch of worms are growing out of your head." (She was right. It did look exactly that way.) "Does Mommy know about this?" she added suspiciously.

"Actually, it was Mommy's idea that I get it done here in LA."

Jordan looked dubious.

Garnet just pointed, speechless. Then he said, "You look like Unka Winsey," referring to his godfather, my friend Lindsay. (I couldn't figure that one out. I saw no physical connection, hair or otherwise.)

Jordan, though, relentlessly cross-examined me from the backseat. "You *really* look different. Why did you do it? I liked you the way you were before. Didn't *you* like yourself the way you were before?" The kid was wielding Thor's hammer, aimed right at my forehead. I ducked.

"Sure," I replied. "I still like myself. But I wanted a different hairstyle. Don't *you* have different hairstyles from time to time?" Her arms were crossed. She wasn't buying it.

They drove off, and I went inside to get myself something to eat.

• • •

Sitting at the table, eating a sandwich, I read that instructional brochure B.J. gave me as I left the salon.

THE EASY WAY TO CARE FOR YOUR TWISTS AND LOCKS

STARTING

When you first start your locks, you should always wear a shower cap when in water. You cannot get your hair wet during the locking process.

CARING FOR YOUR TWISTS OR LOCKS

The hard part in caring for your twists or locks is to leave them alone. If you do not want them to stay locked, just shampoo them out. It takes about six months to a year before your twists are locked in where you can shampoo them as often as you like.

WELL, YOU ARE OFF AND RUNNING AND ON YOUR WAY TO BECOMING HAPPY, NATURAL, AND FREE!

MAINTENANCE

The hair is shampooed once every three to four weeks. We recommend that you sleep on a satin or silk pillowcase, because cotton pillowcases will absorb the natural oils from your hair. During the locking process we suggest that you not put any kind of oils, grease, or sprays on your hair. The hair in its natural state only needs moisture, not oil. We recommend shea butter lotion. Use very little and use it just once a week. Just rub a small amount on hand and smooth across the hair. Only twist the new growth after a good shampoo and condition. Always twist the hair clockwise, the way the hair naturally grows.

SERVICES

Starting Locks—$65.00
Dry Twist—$25.00
Shampoo, Condition, and Retwist—$35.00–$45.00

One thing's for certain: those prices were out of date. *My* "Starting Locks" had cost me *$85*. The bottom line, though, was that while I'd only had them in for about five and a half hours, at that moment it was worth every cent.

• • •

I had another sandwich; I read the *LA Times*. In fact, I lounged grandly around the house for the rest of the evening, a self-satisfied smirk on my face much of the time. I held my magnificent head of hair so erect I was in danger of getting a stiff neck. I did have a difficult moment, though, when, per B.J.'s instructions, I actually put a shower cap over my delicate hair before stepping under the water. I tried to avoid the mirror before opening the shower door. I failed.

Dread Lit Syllabus (iii)

He got out dripping and looking around for shampoo. He was about to give up, not seeing any medicine cabinets, when he accidentally touched a mirror that gave way to reveal shelf upon shelf of bottles among which were several of shampoo boasting placenta protein among their ingredients. The man chose one and stood before the mirror looking at his hair. It spread like layer upon layer of wings from his head, more alive than the sealskin. It made him doubt that his hair was in fact dead cells. Black people's hair, in any case, was definitely alive. Left alone and untended it was like foliage and from a distance it looked like nothing less than the crown of a deciduous tree. He knew perfectly well what it was that had frightened her, paralyzed her for a moment. He could still see those minky eyes frozen wide in the mirror. Now he stuck his head under the shower and wet the hair till it fell like a pelt over his ears and temples. Then he soaped and rinsed, soaped and rinsed until it was as metallic and springy as new wire.

—Toni Morrison, *Tar Baby*, 1981

The Pure (i)

It was around this time that my war with The Pure began.

Even Ivory soap understands that purity is a sham. There's a telling gap between 100 percent pure and 99.44 percent pure. Nothing's pure. Nobody's pure. We're all a jumble of confusing influences, competing factors, and contaminating ideas. Aristotle, in the *Metaphysics*, defines the extremity of a thing as "the first thing outside of which no part is to be found, and the first thing inside of which every part is to be found." How often does *that* occur? Says the *Stanford Encyclopedia of Philosophy*: Aristotle's

> definition is intuitive enough and may be regarded as the natural starting point for any investigation into the concept of a boundary. Indeed, although Aristotle's definition was only meant to apply to material objects, it intuitively applies to events as well...and by extension also to abstract entities such as concepts and sets.

Beware the seekers of purity, beware those who profess purity, for there you will find the hierarchy seekers, those who wish to elevate the clean and sparkling *x* above the dirty, messy, blurry *y*. God, what a boring, lifeless world we'd live in if purity actually existed—where'd the fun be in that?

I wish there was no "but" to follow the above two paragraphs. *But...* I'm all twisted up with The Pure. I have no passport that would allow me to leave The Pure behind, even though I'd love to live elsewhere. For some reason, I strive for The Pure, even though I hate its guts and wish it would leave me alone. Part of my problem, surely, is identity—I love titling, I relish naming and designating, and any such attempt to slap on labels suggests a dalliance with The Pure, on some level, if one digs deep enough. I don't want The Pure around, but every time I turn to escape there it is, all up in my grill—and once I reach out to grab its lapels, it vanishes because, after all, it doesn't really exist.

The Blur trumps The Pure, but no matter: They can't live without each other.

The Pure (ii)

Consider The Pure an incurable disease. I love watching people; I love eavesdropping on strangers' conversations. And what I love most is watching geeks try to resist the geek-face and its accompanying correction—especially since every true geek will always fail. You can see pain, resistance, nervousness, even desperation on a geek's face when the ill-informed begin braying like chimpanzees. Occasionally a geek's hand will wipe a near-sweaty brow or swipe across a mouth, as the geek—the self-aware geek, anyway, and that's no given—tries to resist making the "Well, actually..." correction. Resistance, as our Borg buddies know all too well, is futile.

I had a student in my office a few years ago who was enthusiastically talking about how much he likes zombies. He's a zombie geek. I said, "Oh yeah, like in that Will Smith movie, uh...*Legend*, that's it. Yeah." Halfway through my sentence, I watched, fascinated, as the geek-face clouded over my student's countenance. His eyes darted left and right; he began to shift in his chair; he just couldn't stand the inaccuracy. There we were, student and professor, sitting in my office chatting amiably, when suddenly The Pure appeared wide and tall in the doorway, brushed past the two of us, and grimly, stonily sat down. "Well, actually," the student said, "those aren't zombies. They never died, they just changed form as a result of some virus. Zombies, technically, are people who have died and yet still roam the earth." I smiled knowingly and happily stood corrected. What I loved most about that moment was how familiar it felt, and how wonderful it was to be on the receiving side for a change. The ignorant side. "I love jazz," I occasionally hear people say. "Kenny G is my favorite." Cue *my* geek-face, spreading, like a virus, from temple to chin, from ear to ear. "Well, actually," I can't help but reply, "that's not jazz. What you're describing is instrumental pop. Perfectly wonderful music, if you're into that. But it's not jazz. Sorry. It just isn't." Every now and then I'll hear someone suggest that black hair is narrowly political—that you can tell someone's politics, or at least their approach to life, based on whether she straightens her hair, or whether he's got a short, conservative natural. "Well, actually," I can't resist saying, The Pure grabbing me by the throat, as if to force words from my mouth, "there's simply no explicit causal link between black hair and politics—that's just not the way black hair works." What I don't add is that those sorts of cheap, intellectually lazy ways of looking at black hair are infuriating to those of us who see black hair in all its thick, nappy complexity. Those of us who love it, love every strand of it. Down to the scalp. Down to beneath the scalp. All of it.

Style-ish

Fashion is the realm of the unique. It's uniqueness, but it's also fitting in: that's one of the other paradoxes about it. You have to stand out and you have to fit in. And how you negotiate that tension really defines how fashionable you are.

—Judith Thurman, on *The New Yorker* podcast, May 5, 2014

I began to think more deeply about my clothes. I went to Washington, DC, about a week before Halloween for a Sterling Brown conference. I was staying at my best friend Lindsay's house, and I took the Metro to the Library of Congress and spent the day at the conference. I had wanted to stay for a reading of Sterling Brown's poetry from Yusef Komunyakaa, Sonia Sanchez, Rita Dove, and Michael Harper, poetry legends all, but I was still feeling the lingering effects of almost losing my life a scant few hours earlier on Interstate 95. Four-car pileups will do that. So I eased out of the conference and back to Lindsay's to think things through.

My attempt to find a suitable clothing aesthetic to match my dreadlocks was nothing new, really. The cultural assumptions for dreadlocked people are that they should dress in a style that matches the locks—if they want to be coherent, at least. And why wouldn't coherence be the goal, if there is an attraction to dreadlocks in the first place? I really did think, at first, that I would just keep my clothing aesthetic from before I got twisted, and some small part of me still wanted that. The bigger part, though, wanted me to go all the way out, or at least as far out as I could go and still somehow remain myself.

Surely, I felt different underneath this hair-helmet. This "Sterling A. Brown: American Poet and Cultural Worker" conference was the first time I'd been at an academic event with my head twisted up. And I could see, walking around, other versions of the me I used to be: There were plenty of brothers in coats and ties with short, sharp, closely cropped hair. More "corporate" than "academic"; more "professional" than "professorial," I'd say. But there always was another aesthetic, a different, if not parallel, vibe at conferences like this. This is black academe at the turn of the century, after all, and at conferences or lectures, seminars or symposia, there's usually someone on the scene in dreadlocks, wearing either blatantly Afrocentric or muted "ethnic" garb—or wearing dreadlocks while dressed in all black. I never sensed any animosity between the dread or non-dread camps—I'm not sure either side would even consciously consider themselves in "camps"—but the aesthetic was definitely divergent. And I'd flipped. I was once on one side, and then, after a brief visit to a locktician, I was now on the other side.

I liked it better on the dread side.

It was something like junior high, when I would be eating lunch with white friends while stealing sideways, longing glances across the cafeteria and wishing I was sitting with the black kids. I eventually made that move in high school, and discovered I liked "black" better. But it was during this visit to DC that I began to question—again—what I should wear. Clothes don't talk back as loudly as hair does; at least, not when you're attempting modest changes, anyway. And even though I'd pledged to wear my tie-with-cool-shirt-and-saddle-shoes ensemble all the time, clothing doesn't demand as much of a commitment as hair. It's not like I could wake up one day and decide not to be twisted for a day or two; I couldn't take a week's break from my forced march toward locking. But clothing… let's just say I lagged on occasion. I still wore ties at unconventional, inopportune times, but the *all the time* imperative didn't really happen, after all. I kept backsliding to my previous suburban clothing aesthetic, my comfort zone, even as I struggled to get outside of it. While I was in Washington, I rededicated myself. I began to give it more serious thought.

For the bulk of the conference I was wearing clothing like black corduroy pants and a rust-colored pullover Val had recently bought me. I felt like I looked okay—utterly conventional and boring, but okay, at least, for someone sitting in the audience. But I didn't come here to present anything. What about when I next sat on a panel? I wondered what I would wear then. I wondered, *Could I get away with what I'm wearing today?* And that was, I believe, the first time I doubled back on those words, and wondered just what it meant to use the phrase "get away with"? What does it mean to think in terms of "getting away with" hair and attire? It sounds like I was grappling, yet again, with social conformity norms, but this time in terms of attire.

I decided I would open a negotiation with the sort of clothes people wearing dreadlocks are expected to wear. The problem is that I didn't have a prayer of being able to carry that colorful clothing style off. The knit hat of red, gold, and black? The kufi? The mud cloth? The pajama-like pants? Not gonna happen. Not in a million years. No matter how far I had matured from a bashful junior high school kid who wrestled with finding a stylish clothing combination that didn't make him feel uncomfortable, that kid refused to die. And sometimes he'd roar into the present—and take over.

What are the parameters, the professional-cum-professorial boundaries? Shouldn't I be able to decide for myself whether I'm nestled firmly "in-country," or whether my toe-tips are touching the border?

I had to make some decisions: I wanted to be stylish, but I didn't want to be trendy. And I wasn't at all sure I even wanted to be stylish, except in the strictest sense of the word: I wanted to be "in" style, but not *of* style. I wanted to walk a thin, tightrope line: not stylish, per se, but style-*ish*—both inside and outside of style at the same time, someone who has a recognizable clothing aesthetic, but who doesn't appear to be thinking about style too terribly much at all, something like studied nonchalance—minus the "studied." I decided that I wanted a clothing signature to complement my hair, but one that might oppose my hair, as well: one that confronted and displayed my romance with chaos.

Unfamiliarity

I wasn't used to them; I was a newborn; it was all still very, very novel and bizarre. But there they were, all over my head, and it didn't take long for me to feel the impact getting twisted had on my life—or, at least, the impact I thought they were having on my life.

Even Jordan quickly saw through my mask. Later that week, she turned to me after I'd come downstairs and, with a barely perceptible shrug, said, "I've gotten used to your hair." This after she'd repeatedly called me "Mr. Dreadlock Man" for three straight days since I got twisted. That's all it takes? I wondered. Go figure.

Death Sentence (ii)

I have to deal with the reality that I've gassed the style, smothered it, bludgeoned it beyond recognition. I did this by growing my own dreadlocks and thereby contorting the style beyond its original identity. If dreadlocks was a radio station and had added my locked head to its black hair playlist, it'd be dealing with a serious tune-out factor, because the fledgling song of my hair would be out of balance with the other music in heavy rotation. And if there are too many songs that make listeners switch to another station, the station's ratings fall. Programming heads roll. DJs get fired. The station dies.

If I make the claim that I killed the style—and I do—then I have to deal with time, plain old ordinary historical time. The only way I could know that I've killed dreadlocks is through recognizing when they were born, how and why they lived, and what made them so susceptible to such an untimely death. And I'm not talking about the locks themselves, either. I've written about the literal history of dreadlocks already; that's mostly about hair. This is about culture. I want to grapple with the fast life and hard death of the American dreadlocks phenomenon: how the hairstyle arrived on the shores of the United States—how it was received, how it spread—and how it was viewed, seen, and "read" by the American public, and I want to talk about it by delving, in a deeply personal, completely subjective, and highly idiosyncratic way, into dreadlocks' golden age.

Back to Bob—and Beyond

It's easy enough to say dreadlocks' golden age began with Bob Marley. "By 1976, Bob Marley was a star," writes Stephen Davis in *Bob Marley*. "He had made it. In record parlance, that was the year the Wailers 'broke'; they were in demand for concerts, advance orders for their new album flowed in and *Rolling Stone* magazine voted them 'Band of the Year.' It was the year after *Natty Dread*, and thousands of young Jamaicans had stopped combing their hair and started to think the Rastas were right after all. Their leader was Bob Marley." As such, then, 1976 might be the moment to start dreadlocks' golden age—for Jamaica. But dreadlocks were a few years away from becoming an "age" in the United States. The number of people wearing dreadlocks was too small for that. That's the thing with golden ages: It's partly a numbers game. We might well be living, for example, in a golden age of documentary filmmaking right now. But the only way for us to realize that is when we see a remarkable number, a noticeable number of successful, attention-getting documentaries. One terrific documentary won't make a golden age. Neither will two. But a glut of engaging, gripping nonfiction films prompts critics, viewers, and reviewers alike to look back and see what *wasn't* happening in previous years, then to compare that past with today, and presto: golden age.

But dreadlocks are long past their golden age: "By the 1990s," writes Christopher John Farley in *Before the Legend: The Rise of Bob Marley*, "dreadlocks were everywhere—tucked beneath the caps of baseball players, draped over the furrowed brows of Nobel Prize laureates, tied up behind the ears of political commentators on Fox News. But at first, the hair choices of the Rasta brethren were seen as frightening to children, destabilizing to society, and possibly even sacrilegious." And so yet another irony about dreadlocks is revealed: If too few people wear them, it's pre-golden age; If too many wear them, it's post-golden age. If American dreadlocks were leaden for most of the 1970s, and yet "by the 1990s" they were "everywhere," that must mean that the expanded 1980s were dreadlocks' American golden age.

Golden Age

"A Symbolically Aggressive Profusion of Kinks"

1979

Dreadlocks provoked. It was as simple as that. Once the hairstyle stopped being provocative, the golden age ended. And early on, it wasn't simply the unkempt hairstyle that bothered Americans. After all, it was almost seen as the absence of a hairstyle, an anti-hairstyle, in those early years. No, the main problem was what the hair symbolized for the average American. Those into reggae music likely saw locks as part of the ganja-fueled "natural" Rastafarian lifestyle. But imagine if you knew nothing about reggae other than that it existed at all. And yet you, like millions of other loyal Americans in the pre-cable, pre-internet days of 1979, tuned into *60 Minutes* one Sunday evening and were met with a ringing alarm in the form of a segment on violent Jamaican street gangs. Absent any other context through which to comprehend, on the one hand, Rastafarians and the growing number of Jamaican immigrants, and on the other hand that aggressive, peculiar, and off-putting way some of them wore their hair, that *60 Minutes* segment was the way millions of Americans were introduced to the dreadlock hairstyle.

If the first dread convergence was Jamaica, Haile Selassie, and the Rastafari, and the second dread convergence was, undoubtedly, reggae and Bob Marley, then the third dread convergence was crime, foreign menace, and weird, gross-looking hair. Since the 1970s, the United States had been absorbing the overwhelming majority of the 20,000 Jamaicans who were emigrating annually. Due to reggae's dominant cultural influence in Jamaica, by the early 1980s Rasta-wear was all the rage among Jamaican youth—dreadlocks, I-talk, Rasta colors—and a tiny, particular slice of the migrating Jamaicans brought with them the look, sound, and hair of the Rastafari. But they *weren't* Rastas. This tiny slice were drug addicts and gunmen, and they were motivated to organize drug networks on the mainland, where they felt there was so much demand, so much money to be made.

"Added to this criminal image," writes Barry Chevannes, "was the 'strange' appearance of the dreadlocks. Americans, who had for centuries been used to Africans cropping their hair short and who had just got over the threat of cultural independence represented in the 'Afro' and 'bush' hairstyles, were now confronted with yet another hair statement by blacks: a symbolically aggressive profusion of kinks. Dreadlocks were not only strange (even to African-Americans); they were intimidating as well."

Let's just say, then, that while singing along to songs about Buffalo Soldiers and enjoying a contact high at a reggae concert was a mellow way to become introduced to the dreadlock hairstyle, by the time the 80s arrived, the American mainstream's view of people wearing dreads was all about fear—dread, indeed—of crime and aggression. By the time CBS sounded the warning with its first *60 Minutes* segment in 1979, and followed that with another in December of 1980, numerous Americans who didn't first find out about dreadlocks through the Rastafari or reggae had seen it associated with a fearsome media buzz phrase: the "Jamaican drug posse."

Presumably Jamaican

Keep in mind that dreadlocks had been consciously adopted by the Rastafari to inspire "dread" in everything and everybody not Rasta. And it worked—by 1959 there were tense confrontations with Jamaican police and alarmist media stories about Rastas in the Jamaican press. In the United States, as early as 1971, the *New York Times* was quoting the NYPD, who referred to Rastafarians as violent, uncontrollable cultists who "shoot whoever they feel like."

I know from personal experience about the powerful urge to link dreadlocks with a Jamaican nationality. I was standing with my daughter at the school bus stop one day, and when the bus came she got on. The bus backed up to turn around, so I stepped safely out of the way. What Jordan laughingly told me later was that a helpful female rider, as the bus began to back up, yelled to the bus driver, "Don't run over that Jamaican man!" (To which somebody else immediately responded, "That's Jordan's *dad*!")

Or the time Val and I were scouting an elementary school for Garnet in Worcester. The principal took us around the building, and occasionally we would poke our heads into a room as the teachers taught. We never interrupted the class by saying anything out loud, of course; the principal would open the door and we'd silently stand in the doorway for a few ticks and then move on. When Val got to her office later that morning, she told a woman whose son went to that school that we'd visited her son's class. The next day, Val's coworker came back to their office with a chuckle and a tale: Seems she'd gone home and asked her son if anyone had looked into his classroom that day. (He definitely would have seen us, too; each time the door opened, every single head in every single class had ripped toward us, without exception.) So she asked him, and he said no, no one had.

"Are you sure?" she asked.

He thought for a moment, and then his face brightened. "Oh! A *Jamaican* couple looked in on us today!"

In both instances, I was a silent party—I issued no verbal marker that would fix me as a native United Stateser. I'm sure that if I had been wearing the close-cropped hairstyle I'd worn before getting twisted, I would have been perceived as the adult American black man that I am. I wasn't wearing "Rasta colors" or any other distinctive clothing. But I did have tendrils of hair spiraling out of my head that screamed, in both instances, "Jamaican!" Keep in mind, both times those who made the assumption were relatively innocent young kids. Imagine an older adult who keeps track of the news and heard, over and over in the late 1970s and early 1980s, about scary Rastas with gross, icky hair, probably high on God-knows-what, and liable to "shoot whoever they feel like" at any given moment.

Border Patrol (i)

I think puns get a bad rap. They're not "groaners"; they're not the lowest form of comedy, at least not in my book (get it??). In my house, in my family, puns are elevated to high art. It's the blurring, the double meaning that I find so appealing. I recently took an American Studies seminar on campus with some other professors at the University of Richmond, and one of my colleagues finally returned after missing several meetings. I was told she'd hurt her back shoveling snow. And then one day she reappeared, and…I punned. I couldn't help it. When I saw her, I expressed my concern for her injury— "Laura, your back!" at the very same time and with the very same sounds that I used to welcome her return: "Laura! You're back!" But the words, the sounds, the vocal pitch, the inflection, the enunciation, the intonation—were all completely indeterminate; I was saying two wildly different things at one time with one utterance. Whichever sentence, Laura thought I was using was the one I was using—to her—but the proliferation of meanings remained.

I have no idea why puns are looked down upon by wordsmiths and word-lovers, but I know why I love them. Slapping contemptuously at The Pure, they firmly hold at least two meanings at once—sometimes more, if the rare opportunities for the triple- and quadruple-entendre arise, and I'm always on the lookout. Puns obscure determinate meaning in ways that I deeply appreciate. Don't dreadlocks do something similar? If I'm wearing dreadlocks I'm Jamaican, I'm Rasta, I'm a reggae musician, I'm stinky, I'm a marijuana smoker, I'm bohemian, I'm a drug dealer, I'm creative, I'm countercultural, and I'm messy. Dreadlocks personify chaos. In my book.

Laugh at It. Reduce It. Control It. (i)

1980

What does America do when it's faced with something scary, chaotic, and confrontational? How does America react when it's as "frightened" as Jadine was when she first saw Son's hair in *Tar Baby*? What's the response when America is "paralyzed," with its minky national "eyes frozen wide"?

Laugh at it. Reduce it. Control it. Or, at least, try to. (Think Maynard G. Krebs on *The Many Loves of Dobie Gillis.* Freaked out by those subversive beatniks lurking on the edges of the otherwise vanilla 1950s? Wait a minute: *There's one now*, tiny on your TV screen, and doesn't he seem like such a nice, funny young man?) With the death of Bob Marley in 1981, dreadlocks were in search of an icon to personalize the style. Into that early 80s vacuum various personalities emerged, one of whom was completely fictional. *Fridays*, a short-lived late-night television show on ABC that featured sketch comedy and musical performances, premiered on April 11, 1980, and ran until March 19, 1982. During part of those two-plus seasons, a recurring sketch featured Darrow Igus as a Rastafarian chef. The conceit of the sketch is that no matter what he cooks, it has to be liberally seasoned with ganja. As the sketch became popular, it grew into an audience-interaction crowd-pleaser, as the chef would ask the audience what that chief ingredient was: "Is it turmeric?" And the audience would chant along with him, "No, no, NOOO, no..." Until the chef finally yelled, "Gimme GANJA!!!" And the audience would scream, "Yeah, yeah, YEAHHHHH, yeah!"

I laughed. It was funny, if not terribly clever. I remember, especially, when the character would appear as "Rasta Claus" and similarly chant the popular taglines, all the while employing the four verbal and visual cues one would expect of someone playing a Rastafarian character whose name happened to be "Nat E. Dred": Jamaican accent, multiple references to marijuana, colorful Rasta clothes, and, of course, dreadlocks—in this case a dreadlock wig. Oh yeah, I laughed. I would yell, "No, no, NO, no..." and, at the proper moment, I would holler, "Yeah, yeah, YEAH, yeah!" I love that sort of audience participation, particularly when I get to play along. I had fun, but I was also being educated. It was an introduction for some viewers, and a confirmation for others. Images have power, particularly when dealing with a barely known culture such as the Rastafarians. I have little doubt that far more people saw Nat E. Dred on a single night of a *Fridays* broadcast than the total number of Americans who ever saw Bob Marley onstage.

It didn't really matter if viewers had a preliminary understanding of Rastafarian beliefs or not; the sketch roared into our consciousness, regardless, and lodged itself there, embedded in our heads, ready to be referenced whenever someone in dreadlocks appeared in front of us, or anywhere in the media, for that matter. Was it an innocent sketch that shouldn't be taken seriously? Perhaps. But to deny its cultural power is foolish, particularly at a time when ideas and concepts like "Rastafarian" and "dreadlocks" were free-floating signifiers—at least in America—waiting to be anchored and grounded in a specific context. Was it extremely harmful? No, no, NO, no. But did it matter culturally? Yeah, yeah, YEAH, yeah.

Call and Response

It was a little like being pregnant. Or what I imagined it would be like to be pregnant. During the aftermath of getting twisted, I realized the true extent to which growing dreadlocks stood out—literally. Simply put, dreadlocks place you squarely under the microscope of a huge, unblinking public eye. People tend to view dreadlocks, even twists, dreads-in-training, like they view pregnant women: as somehow part of the public domain. I once heard a man on some television talk show tell the story of the very last time he poked a pregnant woman in the stomach. He'd apparently done it many times before, just handled a woman's body; he said he liked to playfully poke them in the belly with his index finger while making some crack, some smart remark. Well, this last time, with finger extended, he pushed into the belly of a total stranger. And instead of resistance, instead of feeling a taut, melon-like membrane housing human life, his finger kept going. Confused, he pushed in, much farther than ever before. But she wasn't pregnant—she was overweight. He was chagrined; she was embarrassed; he was cured of that stupidity forever. But that's just one example of how people take liberties with pregnant women. They ask them questions that shouldn't be asked, they make comments that shouldn't be made—all because late-term pregnancy simply cannot be hidden. The very tall, the very short, the obese, and the handicapped among us feel, I have no doubt, something similar. As do the dreadlocked among us. People stare, total strangers make comments, children point, their mouths agape and eyes wide. People I barely know ask about my personal life. It's usually fun; occasionally it's exasperating—I guess it depends on my mood. I don't really mind it, but I can understand how it might become difficult for people who value their privacy to the extreme. Hair talks. It's a nonverbal "call." And, in the case of dreadlocks, it certainly does invite—it almost demands—a "response."

A Thick, Matted Rorschach Test

I've always felt that the best way to observe a beautiful woman is to not look at her. I mean, sure, I do look at her, because she's beautiful and I want to enjoy the aesthetic beauty of the human form, the same way I'd want to look at a beautiful sunset or a gorgeous painting or a dazzling house or car or an extremely handsome or interesting-looking man, for that matter. But since I watch beautiful women, I've always felt that the best way to do it is by not looking at her, but by looking at the men around her. I love watching women through the eyes of men. I've seen longing, I've seen deep pleasure in men's eyes as they watch a stunning woman. More than once I've seen a man eye a woman's torso as if he thinks he can read words written on her body underneath her clothes.

I found myself using that strategy in order to watch my hair. I couldn't see my hair, of course—it was on top of my head, and my eyes, obviously, were looking out. So the only way I could see my hair was to watch the reaction of the people looking at me. The only problem was that I often forgot I was wearing the hairstyle. In the same way a beautiful woman might sort of forget she's beautiful until some leering jerk makes a point of reminding her, I was reminded that I was wearing an unusual hairstyle by the looks I'd get when people reacted to my hair.

It put me in mind of when I was young and I used to torture my little brother, in the sorts of ways that big brothers do, by staring just above his head. It drove him crazy, so of course I kept doing it. Soon enough, I had trained myself: Don't look at his face, look above his face; don't look into his eyes, look inches above his eyes, over his head, and wait patiently until he dissolves. And now, in a kind of karmic reversal, people were doing it to me—only they weren't staring at the space just above my crown, they were staring at the angry tangle of hair growing out of my head like black lanyard. It's almost as if dreadlocks were a thick, matted Rorschach test; people looked at them and projected onto them what they would:

Riding northbound on the San Diego Freeway in the passenger seat of my college friend Keith's Volvo...

> "I always wanted to do that," he admitted, glancing up at my hair as he accelerated slightly, the rush-hour traffic as tight as the naps on an uncombed head. "But see, it might disturb business. I'm a mortgage broker, man; I have to go into people's homes," he explained, as if dreadlocks were a communicable disease, as if potential clients, fearing contamination, would shout at him to go away from behind locked doors.

Sitting in the audience at Holman United Methodist Church on Adams Boulevard in Los Angeles later that same day, waiting for Toni Morrison to come out and read from Paradise...

> A friend of my sister relentlessly interrogated me: *Who did it? How much did it cost? How long did it take? How is it maintained?* and much, much more. I enjoyed the conversation; I liked talking about my hair. I knew before I got twisted that I wouldn't be one of those people who think they can walk around with the equivalent of a bloody human eyeball pinned to their lapel and then have the nerve to get upset when someone asks, "Why do you have a bloody human eyeball pinned to your lapel?" It was as if these

reticent eyeball-bearers believed the gesture somehow explained itself. I knew that some people weren't going to care about my hair, and some people were going to care, even if it was just barely enough to ask about it. And I knew some people would care a lot. I was happy to tell her what I knew, as early in the game as it was, but I did wonder if a trend had started here, what with the number of envy-fueled I-always-wanted-to-do-that-too responses I'd received in the first few days after getting twisted.

Standing at a railing at the Getty Museum, moments after finishing lunch with my sister, looking out over western Los Angeles…

We were silent for a moment, then I said, "Wanna peek inside my head?"

"What?" she said sharply, unsure she'd heard me properly.

"Would you like to peek inside my head?" I repeated. "Picture a man standing on a rooftop, hollering loudly, with both hands buried in his hair, and he's scratching, scratching, scratching as if he's hearing voices inside his head tell him he'd better not ever stop. Then he climbs down, sighing with relieved satisfaction."

Pam listened, continuing to look at the view.

"Or imagine a naked man balled up on the floor in the corner of an otherwise empty room, and his fingernails are busy, frantically scratching, scratching, scratching his scalp. Then he stretches wide on the floor, smiling and exhaling with relief."

"Let me guess," said Pam, sighing. "You'd like to scratch your hair."

• • •

On the third day, he began to itch.

• • •

The question, it seemed to me, was whether I could make it a whole month without scratching. The itching wasn't really bad when it started, but then again, it wasn't really hot then, either. I wondered what it would be like when it got good and filthy up there on top of my head. What would happen when summer heated up my oily scalp and I was still only two or three weeks into it, weeks away from my scheduled shampoo…? Well, by then I just knew I was going to be a wild man. I was going to go insane.

Now, I did bring an inflation needle with me to the museum. I had purchased it a few days earlier to inflate a basketball for Garnet. And I brought it with me to the Getty, just in case the urge to scratch became unbearable. Something like a smoker who was trying to quit smoking but hid emergency cigarettes because, well, you never know. B.J. said an inflation needle was something I could use if I absolutely had to scratch, if I just couldn't hold out. It would satisfy the itch, but wouldn't mar the twist.

I never used it; I didn't scratch that day. I wanted to learn how to stand it. I wanted to learn how to deal with the constant impulse to scratch, and if I went for the needle that early, I'd never learn to ignore it. I would never learn to confront—and deny—the impulse. So I didn't use the needle. But I knew I was going to have to get over that urge. And soon.

Either way, I said to Pam, "I'm not going to scratch. B.J. said not to, and so I won't. I'm just going to ignore it, or pretend to ignore it, or just find a way to outlast it." I was determined.

Let's Hear It for the Boy

1982

Some people simply called him the Boy. Most knew him as Boy George, a white Londoner with a beautiful falsetto who possessed what one commentator called a "femme-fatale face," featuring "plucked, penciled eyebrows, mascaraed and shadowed eyes, pancaked and blushed skin, and tart-bright lipstick." Boy George became an international star in 1982 with Culture Club's first hit, "Do You Really Want to Hurt Me?," a reggae-influenced pop tune. One might think the Boy's wearing of dreadlocks, combined with the sound of reggae in his breakout hit, might lead to the widespread adoption of the style. It didn't. While his gender-fluid persona prompted a brief fashion trend in the early 80s, he didn't appear to influence American style, let alone black American style, very much; maybe the significance of his dreadlocks was lost in his overall culture clash. Maybe his whiteness prevented blacks from seeing his dreadlocks as culturally viable. Whatever it was, as Peter Buckley put it in *The Rough Guide to Rock*, "The sight of this strapping six-footer mincing across the stage in white smock and dreadlocks caused much raising of eyebrows, but it represented an instant success story, which would burn itself out almost as quickly."

"Nat E. Dred" and Boy George were both, in their own ways, cultural phenomena—Nat Dred a transitory, mini-phenomenon at best, and the Boy a dominant, if brief-lived, pop music figure of the early 80s. Both, however, called to mind that familiar dreadlock troika of reggae, Rasta and Jamaica. For me, though, the first time I clearly recall seeing dreadlocks on someone who was not Jamaican, not Rastafarian and not a reggae musician was, predictably enough, in connection with a man accused of a crime.

"the intense negronis, of my revolutionary hair"

1983

I couldn't take my eyes off the screen. I was visiting Los Angeles from San Jose, sitting on the couch, watching Edward Lawson's press conference from our rumpus room in the house in which I'd grown up, and neither earthquakes, thunderstorms, nor loud explosions in the street outside could have interrupted my attention. The man was striking, and I was riveted. If there was one single, signal moment that watered the tiny seed of dread that hearing about Yvonne's brother had planted in my head, that was it. Lawson, wearing a blindingly white suit, stood tall before the microphones and cameras: no grin, no laughs, just an unassailable outraged dignity that made his locks seem like they only enhanced his bearing. What's more, he was furious, and is there anything more compelling—to whites, to blacks, to America, to the world—than black rage? As I remember it, he kept stressing that all he was doing was walking—and that simply walking had led him to stand before the cameras. The *Los Angeles Times* described him this way: "a tall, black man with shoulder length braids or 'dreadlocks.'"

In the eighteen months leading up to 1975, Edward Lawson was arrested more than fifteen times under California's vagrancy laws, which, in terms of how these were enforced, amounted to Lawson being arrested simply for the "crime" of walking through affluent neighborhoods in the San Diego area. He sued, claiming that it was unconstitutional for cops to demand identification, and by 1983 his case had reached the United States Supreme Court, where he won his case—arguing the case himself before the court wearing dreadlocks, likely an American first—and California's vagrancy laws were overturned. The resulting media attention landed him on television nationwide.

Up to that moment, I don't believe I'd ever seen dreadlocks on anyone except Jamaicans and reggae musicians. If I had, I have no recollection of it. But I certainly noticed them on Edward Lawson. When he stepped to the bank of microphones, I'm sure my eyebrows furrowed, my head tilted slightly, and my eye-camera zoomed and refocused until a close-up of his locks filled the screen of my mind. It was my first experience of lock lust, something I never knew existed until that moment. His dreadlocks were as striking as one can imagine they would be, given the scarcity of the hairstyle at the time. I'm reminded of archival photographs I've seen of similarly angry young black men wearing Afros, black leather jackets, and dark shades at press conferences in the late 1960s. I had just turned 24 years old in the spring of 1983—myself a young, if not terribly angry, black man—and my reaction to the coded messages Edward Lawson's appearance sent out at that spring press conference was as visceral as one might imagine. I realize now that I was deeply moved. I was altered for all time.

I was struck, as well, by the fact that he was wearing both dreadlocks and that longtime bastion of Western respectability, a suit, although as I recall he was wearing a T-shirt and not a tie. He was, and still is, an activist, and he's apparently a style warrior, as well. Lawson was one of those early dread-setters who, alone among wearers of the style I've talked to or read about, did not first see dreadlocks on someone else: "when i started wearing my hair, as such, i had never heard of dreads, nor had anyone else in america," he wrote to me in an all lowercase e-mail.

> i can remember in the 60s stopping traffic, by just walking on the campus of the black howard university or causing a bus crash in chicago by the intense negronis, of my revolutionary hair. or i can remember appearing in newspaper photos, where the embarrassed house negroes, simply gave my photo a cut. i started wearing my hair [in dreadlocks] in the early 1960s. you cannot even begin to imagine the dimensions of [this] issue in negro hair america. my life has been a study of hair and self-hatred in negro america, with more stories than there are hairs on my head.

Well, I do believe I can begin to imagine the dimensions of "negro hair in america," but what I can't imagine is the reaction to wearing hair in a style we now know as dreadlocks *in the early 1960s*, an era when just wearing an Afro was stepping way, way outside. Lawson, presuming he's accurate in his description, wore locks before Bob Marley, at a time when they were absolutely without precedent in this country. I have no doubt his hair were antennae, attracting attention—and trouble—in equal measure.

And yet, even Lawson begins to fit the dread profile when he reveals why he grew his hair:

> for someone who was an individual," he wrote, "it was an off the cuff, casual, living question: what would happen to a negro, if i stopped combing and cutting my hair? no negro had ever dared to even ask such a question, for fear that the lord would strike you down with a curling iron, and fling your mortal soul into the burning pit [of] concolene (pre jerry [sic] curl) for eternity. decades later, i am still unraveling the answer everyday.

Victorious Exile

1983

I only recall still images of the tournament, in those dark ages before ESPN took off, but the photographs showed a light-skinned black man, his tennis racquet outstretched, collar-length locks splayed from his head like so many long, slim fingers. One month after Edward Lawson's May 1983 press conference, Yannick Noah won the French Open. It was a big deal, since he was the first Frenchman to do so since 1946. His hair didn't make quite the same impression on me as Lawson's, but I do recall hearing, stateside, the clamor the French made over his win. His playboy reputation didn't hurt his outsized persona, and I remember hearing that he finally had to flee the country because he couldn't walk the streets in peace.

A Signal Moment in the Recent, Post-Afro History of Black Hair in America

1984

Whoopi Goldberg had no problem walking the streets before her off-Broadway run of *The Spook Show*; nobody had any idea who she was. But two seconds onstage changed everything. Of the five characters in *Whoopi Goldberg*, her one-woman Broadway show that began the previous year as *The Spook Show*, the most intriguing is a self-conscious, six-year-old African-American girl who arrives onstage with a white shirt on her head. "This is my long, luxurious blonde hair," the girl announces; she also covets blue eyes to match. You see, she urgently wants to be on *The Love Boat*, but, she stresses, "you have to have long hair." As the moment slowly plays out, several layers of visual possibilities are at work onstage. Whoopi convincingly brings to life the simple image of a little black girl pretending to have long, blonde hair; most telling is the way the girl repeatedly whips her hairlike shirt around and around and from side to side, enjoying its length and body. It's the sort of easily recognizable, rampant hair-flipping that calls to mind beach movies and Barbarella and young, blonde coeds running slow-motion through amber waves of grain, of Prell commercials with silky hair spilling over a naked shoulder, and also my two young cousins at the Smith Family Reunion. What makes the scene so compelling in *Whoopi Goldberg* is that the girl does *not* have long hair—no explicit hair weaves, no extensions, no permanent, no straightening of any sort. The kid's got a shirt on her head. She's pretending. But she's doing so in a culturally specific fashion, and it's impossible to ignore the influence, as we watch, of America's prevailing European beauty aesthetic—even though the words "European beauty ideal" are, obviously, never uttered by this young child. Then, partway through the monologue, the girl snatches the shirt from her head. She says her mother has told her, "I ought to be happy with what I got, but see"—and she rips the shirt away, pauses briefly, and says, "it don't *do* nothin'."

It was, as one might imagine, a moment.

As an audience we "see" a little girl's nappy head of hair. Still firmly encased in the fictional reality of the scene, the shirt has been removed, but all the viewer "sees" is whatever representation of short, kinky, Negroid hair each individual member of the audience can *imagine*, based on previously received, formerly viewed images of uncombed black hair. While individuals who make up an audience always view events onstage through their own specific reality, in this case they are literally required to project their personal, historical sense of what kinky black hair looks like in order to "see" that little girl's hair at all. And what's most interesting is that the head of hair we're *actually* looking at during that scene is, of course, Whoopi's own dreadlocks. I can't vouch for anyone else who views that scene, but as I watched, that little girl's nappy head morphed into Whoopi's dreadlocked head and back again countless times throughout the two seconds that an impish Whoopi stands there, mischievously, wordlessly grinning at the audience. I see that image—Whoopi onstage, in character, standing silently beneath her hair—as a signal moment in the recent, post-Afro history of black hair in America.

The moment is a controlling metaphor for the way hair "speaks" for Whoopi, the way it marks an unconventional persona that is difficult, if not impossible, to define. As she stands alone onstage, after literally telling them to "look!", she seems to be almost daring her audience to "read" black hair for all its symbolic complexity, to see it for what it *does* "do." In character and out, European beauty ideal literally bunched in her hand in the form of a white shirt, she dances in and around and on minstrelsy and militancy, conventionality, and unacceptability, recalling black icons as disparate as Topsy and Marley—and Pecola in *The Bluest Eye*. Massive cultural queries and notions and impulses buzzed on, around, and through that character's hair as if it were a busy airport hub in bad weather: some landing, some unable to land, some unable to take off, some just circling warily. Those electrically charged two seconds contained black hair's historical references, political implications, stylistic possibilities, stylistic impossibilities, dreams, fantasies, nightmares, and resistances.

The moment symbolized the arrival, for me, anyway, of the golden age of America's dreadlock hairstyle. All that came before then was just the clearing of cultural throats before Whoopi began to sing. As her multiracial audience gazed up at her, Whoopi framed and then presented her intertwined, matted hair follicles to her viewers to make of them what they would. There was no singular, ready-made, American political ideology that grew out with her locks. Those two seconds symbolically encapsulated all of the possibilities that were to characterize her topsy-turvy, thrill ride of a career since then—a career that, it might be argued, could not have existed in exactly the same way if she had tried to launch it 30, 20, perhaps even 10 years earlier.

"Professorial." (ii)

Standing in the living room of the house where I grew up, near Mr. Howard, a family friend, as he flipped through photos my mother took at my graduation ceremony in May…

"Now *here* he looks like a professor," he said, staring down at a photo of me with graying temples—before I got twisted.

Sitting outside, at a sidewalk restaurant on Pine Square in Long Beach, California, smoking cigars with Mark, an old friend from high school…

"You look like a professor, Bert," he said. "I'm telling you, I like the dreads, man. Makes you look, I don't know… professorial."

Then: "I can't believe this is your first cigar, 'B.' I figured you'd be smoking cigars by now…"

Wait for it; wait for it… Now:

"…or at least a pipe or something…"

(The classroom door opens at exactly the appointed hour. The professor enters. He's wearing spectacles, loafers, a buttoned-down Oxford shirt, a silk tie, a tweed coat—with elbow patches—and wool slacks. He speaks in a clipped and proper accent, with manner to match, occasionally clearing his throat in a particularly elegant manner. He stands stiffly before his students, nose pointed toward the ceiling, and, before he begins lecturing on the assigned poet, he pauses briefly to light his pipe—as graying dreadlocks tumble about his neck and shoulders!? Hmmmmm…)

Fuzzy Phase (i)

Standing at the bathroom mirror, a scowl on my face...

My hair sucks.

At least, I thought, it sucked as far as I could tell. I was trying to figure out why I didn't like it. Saturday night, hanging out with Mark, I had been in heaven. I loved the way my dreads-in-training lay on my scalp, just so. I was, remember, fresh from both B.J.'s inaugural twist on Tuesday and her retwist earlier that Saturday afternoon. My hair looked exactly the way I wanted it to look. I wish I could have frozen it in place. Because by late July, just a few days after coming back to Worcester, my head looked like a blurry, annoyingly out-of-focus movie. The individual strands—not the twists themselves but the tiny, particular hairs that were gathered up and rotated into twists—were loose and roaming all over my head, as if they were restless, as if they'd suddenly gotten wanderlust. I looked awful. I accosted Val in the kitchen, complaining bitterly: "Look at my hair, Val—what is this?"

She smiled reassuringly. "Well, they're dreadlocks, aren't they? Surely you don't expect neat dreadlocks? They're supposed to be fuzzy, right?"

Well, yes, of course she was right. But still, the fact was, some dreadlocked heads looked better than others. And right now, my hair looked as if it couldn't decide whether it wanted to be dread or not. It looked, well, dreadful. And I had an interview at Brown University for a visiting professorship midday Wednesday. I needed to set up an appointment with someone at Roots 'n Locks so I could get twisted on Wednesday morning. This meant I'd also be testing Roots 'n Locks for future hair maintenance. They were closed on Monday, though. So either they'll have an opening, I thought, or I'll just have to float to Providence naked as I am.

• • •

I finally figured out why my hair looked so shabby. I touched it! B.J. emphatically told me that I was not to touch my hair, and her brochure said something similar. And I hadn't—all day long. It was itching like a rabid rash, too, and still, I had faithfully left it alone.

The night before, like a lunatic, like an idiot, I had placed a baseball jersey over my pillow and then tossed and turned on it all night long. Roughed up my hair but good. The woman expressly said not to touch it. The whole time I had been in LA, I used a pillow wrapped in silk, thanks to a blouse my mother let me borrow. Here, I apparently thought I could withstand the equivalent of rubbing my head with a scratchy polyester baseball jersey for six or seven hours straight. I might as well have used my fingers to scratch it—hard (at least I would have gotten some satisfaction, some release, if I had).

I'll have to suffer through tomorrow, I complained to myself, get twisted the day after that, and then go back to doing what I did in LA. I may have to learn a whole new way of sleeping, but I'd rather do that than walk around with this hazy mess on top of my head. After all, I thought to myself, not only do I have that Brown interview on Wednesday, but I'm also lecturing on campus Thursday. I've got to look better than this.

"Ona MOVE!"

1985

With fears of Jamaican drug posses still very much alive,

events in Philadelphia in the spring of 1985 were coming to a violent head. The MOVE organization was founded in Philadelphia in 1972 by Vincent Leaphart, who adopted the name John Africa, and Donald Glassey, a white college professor and antiwar activist. MOVE members, among other things, ate raw food, believed in physical exercise, and didn't cut their hair, because uncombed hair was the "natural" way to live, as well. I have no idea whether they called their hair "dreadlocks" or not—*Washington Post* reporter Bill Peterson felt it necessary to explain that MOVE members "wore uncombed hair in long, stiff braids called dreadlocks," suggesting that the style was still nowhere near common enough to refer to without explanation—but their uncombed hair would have been characterized as dreadlocks by anyone who was familiar with the style. It lent them a certain unhinged, if uniform, quality, and since the style was still relatively rare at the time, they stood out in the west Philly neighborhood in which they lived. Their hair had grown fairly long by the summer of 1978, when the group had a shootout with Philadelphia police in the Powelton Village section of the city and an officer was killed.

The bookend dates, then, had been established: Between August 8, 1978, and May 13, 1985, whether you were "ona MOVE" (as the group described its members) or not, if you lived in Philadelphia and wore your hair in dreadlocks, you might well have suffered at least seven years, three months, and a week of intense distrust from both black and white residents who were wary of MOVE, and some unwanted attention—to say the least—from the Philadelphia police force. This is the "control it" aspect of the way America reacted to dreadlocks, in the most literal and explicit fashion. If it's hard to imagine being Edward Lawson as his hair attracted attention in the early 60s in Washington, DC and Chicago, it's even harder to fathom wearing dreadlocks in Philadelphia during the MOVE years. At a glance, Philly residents would likely assume anyone wearing locks was a MOVE member, and that assumption would likely prompt an unhappy encounter. Philadelphia police already had an established reputation for being one of the most aggressive and repressive forces in the country. The death of one of their own didn't help matters when it came to how they saw black folk wearing lengthy locks. To wear dreadlocks in Philly in those years, writes "Professor Kim" Pearson in her blog "Professor Kim's News Notes," "was to invite police scrutiny and an occasional beat-down."

On May 13, 1985, gunfire was exchanged on the MOVE compound. That's the day Mayor Wilson Goode ordered the bombing of the MOVE house on Osage Avenue, killing 6 adults and 5 children and destroying 61 houses in the neighborhood. Two years later, *Frontline* documented the events leading up to that Philadelphia fire, and watching the program, even from today's vantage point, is a disturbing experience. The makers of the documentary didn't directly refer to or mention the MOVE members' hair one single time, and why would they? Unlike the necessarily descriptive nature of written narrative, we viewers could see for ourselves what MOVE members looked like.

Unsettling and tragic as the film was, I found myself, almost against my will, mesmerized by the hair of certain MOVE members: Delbert Africa, in particular, was interviewed in prison about the 1978 confrontation, and the camera recorded a magnificent, shoulder-length head of hair with various sizes of locks soldered thickly to his head. His passionate denunciation of the Philly police, and his views on the events of the Powelton Village incident, were made all the more striking by the sight of his dreadlocks.

But it is the almost unbelievably full hair of Ramona Africa that stands out the most. She must be one of those people who just have really dense, extremely thick hair, because the sheer size of her collected locks was an absolute wonder to behold. Her sad eyes, when they weren't flashing with anger, seemed even sadder, and her longish, attractive face seemed even longer between the thickest, widest locks I've ever seen. Her hair, as she speaks on-screen, threatens to envelope her face altogether.

I remember well when Goode dropped the bomb (when talking about the MOVE tragedy, go-go music fans of the day couldn't help ruefully punning on the song "Drop the Bomb" by Trouble Funk; I heard the reference more than once), but seeing how it all began and ended was a shattering experience. I couldn't help but think of how that signal hairstyle MOVE members wore did, indeed, communicate "dread" to everyone outside of MOVE. Although MOVE has nothing whatsoever to do with Rastafarianism, there was a curious, motivational parallel between Youth Black Faith era Rastafarians and those MOVE members. Intentionally or not, MOVE's hairstyle screamed an antisocial message almost as loudly as the loudspeakers they attached to their houses in west Philly. Both messages frightened neighbors, isolated members, and helped identify the people in MOVE, for better or worse, to everyone else in the city. And yet, surely there were people who were wearing dreadlocks who were mistaken for MOVE members and treated accordingly. And make no mistake, some black folks—MOVE's immediate neighbors, for instance—might have welcomed the issuance of such a beat-down.

Back to Whoopi—and Beyond

1985

So what does America do when it's faced with something scary and confrontational? The Afro weirded people out in the 60s; back then America associated basket naturals with young, black "militants" of the day like H. Rap Brown, Huey P. Newton, and, especially, Angela Davis. Whenever I imagine people reacting to the title of Julius Lester's 1969 book, *Look Out, Whitey! Black Power's Gon' Get Your Mama!*, I always visualize "Black Power" as some rough brothers in Black Panther-wear with thick hair reaching for the skies. But by the end of the 70s, the Afro had been so defanged that a rainbow Afro wig on a white guy holding a "John 3:16" sign at sporting events became almost as enduring an icon of the hairstyle as black pop groups like the Sylvers, the Brothers Johnson, and the mighty Jackson 5.

In the 1980s, the American dreadscape was strewn with Jamaican drug posses, frightening Rastas, and at least one group of dreadlocked urban outcasts in Philadelphia. How would America at large respond to yet another black hairstyle that seemed to throw all of her most cherished values up in her face? Well, Toni Morrison, among others, has argued that if there were no black people, America would have had to invent them. And so, in the midst of a decade that began by suggesting that crime and dreadishment go together like the title of a novel, the mid-80s American imagination invented... Whoopi Goldberg.

Yes, people like Alice Walker and ex-NFL star Ricky Williams will tell you that it was Bob Marley who led them to wear dreadlocks, and I believe them. By no means am I ignoring vanguard dread-wearers like the late Jean-Michel Basquiat who, for some early adopters, was as much of an inspiration as Marley. I completely believe people who say Marley and Basquiat were far more of an influence than Whoopi.

But it was Whoopi, in my humble opinion, who gave Middle America—white and black—a model for people wearing dreadlocks as more than Rastas, reggae musicians, criminals, and addicts. Her stage show did produce those fascinating two seconds on Broadway, but people in Peoria didn't know or care about that. Most people first heard of Whoopi when she starred in *The Color Purple* in 1985. She certainly didn't wear dreadlocks in that movie. But thanks to the explosion of cable channels and the ramping up of an American fascination with the private lives of celebrities, people from Peoria to Poughkeepsie were introduced to Whoopi as a personality in her own right—and she was rocking dreadlocks hard as they got to know her.

Whoopi wearing dreadlocks complicated any easy assumptions Americans might have had about people who wore dreadlocks. It was Whoopi, beginning in 1985, who gradually gave black Americans what might be called cultural permission to wear dreadlocks, however unconsciously they might have perceived that permission. And she did it by establishing a context around the hairstyle that had nothing to do with

Jamaica, reggae, or the Rastafari. According to *Essence* magazine, it was actress Rosalind Cash who introduced Whoopi to the style. (There is always *someone* whom a dreadlock wearer sees that leads her to want to wear the style.) I believe she cleared the way for a more complicated public reaction to dreadlocks. Gradually, her enormous fame gave dreadlocks a certain odd, quirky normalcy that allowed for—or, at least, coincided with—the flourishing of the hairstyle. Whoopi was the first dreadlocked mainstream personality, the first Really Big Star to move through America's recognizable media channels with her trademark locks blazing out from her head. The bottom line, for me, is this: If Bob Marley had been truly influential in a mainstream media way, the explosive growth of dread in the USA might well have happened in the 70s. But it didn't happen in the 70s. It happened in the 90s. I believe thousands of dread-worthy African Americans were, consciously or unconsciously, gradually led by Whoopi to see the style as something available for *them*.

"But nature had nothing to do with it!"

1985

It wasn't just Whoopi who was in the American dreadlock vanguard. Imagine an early 80s cultural triangle with "criminal" (Jamaican drug posse) at one point, and "clown" (Nat E. Dred) at another. The third point would represent the subtle but undeniable growth of dreadlocks as an expression of black pride. If the bipolar perception of dreadlock-wearers as either clown or criminal (an uncomfortable but uncanny mirroring of the way America somehow manages to see black men as both the menacing, violent buck and the harmless Sambo buffoon at the very same time), black Americans began to conceive of dreadlocks as an elemental part of African heritage. *Essence* magazine, in particular, has run more than one article in which dreadlocks were heralded as an essential African cultural legacy. Then-NBA player Etan Thomas's poem "My Heritage" is a good example, appearing in *Essence* in 2006 replete with references to dreadlocks being placed upon his head "like an /African crown," after which he stands "proud as a king /A warrior."

But dreadlocks-as-heritage doesn't quite work for me. "Even more so than dreadlocks, there was nothing particularly African about the Afro at all," writes Kobena Mercer in "Black Hair/Style Politics." "Neither style had a given reference point in existing African cultures, in which hair is rarely left to grow 'naturally.'" Mercer insists that however strongly these styles "expressed a desire to 'return to the roots' among black peoples in the diaspora, in Africa as it is they would speak of a 'modern' orientation." And yet, as more and more blacks grew dreadlocks, they did so by appreciating it as "natural," as a style that reflected black pride, and that stance only seemed to grow, just as the Afro-as-heritage stance grew in the 1960s. "But nature had nothing to do with it!" retorts Mercer. "Both these hair-styles were never just natural, waiting to be found: they were stylistically cultivated and politically constructed in a particular historical moment as part of a strategic contestation of white dominancc and the cultural power of whiteness."

Nature vs. "Nature" (iii)

Well, I met Nicole, of Roots 'n Locks. She originally told me noon Wednesday was the earliest she could twist me up, but since that was exactly the time I was scheduled to appear at the English department chair's house in Providence, I asked her if she could squeeze me in earlier, and 3:30 Tuesday was what she came up with. I'll tell you what: B.J. is either clairvoyant or she just flat knows her business. Here, once again, is The Law, as laid down by B.J.: "No beeswax. No sort of gel. Nothing." Period. "Just water. Always twist them wet. Don't twist them yourself." She knew that hairdressers would want to dump chemicals on me once I left the safety of the Global Village. "Don't let them put that stuff in your hair, Bert," B.J. had said, again and again. "You don't want that."

But Nicole wanted that. It's what she knew, same as her fellow headmate, Michelle, who motioned for me to get into her chair when I arrived. Michelle was about my age. Her hair was fairly conventional for a hairdresser, straightened and swept up in the back. On the counter next to her chair was a photo of four boys, and she confirmed that yes, they were all hers. But Michelle was nowhere close to the sort of Chatty Cathy hair salons are known for. Her busy, intelligent eyes made it clear that there was far more going on in her head than she ever let out of her mouth. From my seat in Michelle's chair, I watched Nicole giving a woman a perm. With her platinum blonde short Afro, I wouldn't have guessed that too many of Nicole's clients came in asking for her hairstyle. That day she had worn tight jeans on her compact body, with black lipstick, a screaming red T-shirt, and an appealing, casual nonchalance. She never hurried, she never raised her voice, she never got excited. And she was busy—scheduling appointments over the phone, conferring with a contractor on some work being done, finishing with one client while welcoming another. It was her shop, and she didn't just own the place, she ran the place. But no matter what she did, a soft, slight sigh seemed to accompany it. She was cool.

And so was the shop. It was downtown, in an older, which is not to say historic, building. It rested on a moderately busy corner, a block west of Main Street. Two plate glass windows faced each street, near the door, and I enjoyed watching Worcester walk by as Michelle twisted. Downtown characters drifted past the shop or occasionally popped inside. But before we got started, Michelle and I began to talk. Before long, Nicole turned from pasting baby hair to the forehead of the woman in her chair and, looking puzzled, joined our conversation.

"Water?" Michelle was repeating to me. "That's all? Just water?"

"That's it," I said, confidently. "Water. Just use water to twist it up, and it'll dread on its own. I don't want to use beeswax or any of that other stuff."

They looked at each other, frowning. I knew what they were thinking. It was some variation of this: *You know, the relationship between a hairdresser and a head of hair would be so much easier if we could just do the hair without having to deal with the head underneath.* The hairdresser-client relationship is similar, I think, to the writing professor-student relationship. I'm the professor, and I know what's best for my composition students, but I also know that they must navigate that "best" territory themselves, or else they risk getting lost in the woods when I'm not around. The problem is that difficult space of time during which I issue writing assignments and conduct class meetings in order for them to "discover" what's best for them, particularly when they're committed to staying within their safety zone and writing the way they always have. It's a painful process, because I have to convince them of a better approach to writing without simply saying, "Do it. Because I say so. Because I'm the professor." That approach would work well for exactly the amount of time I am their professor, and then they'd likely go straight back to doing what they always did. But if I can manage to get them to discover for themselves why they're so much better off doing it my way, then they retain it—because it's theirs, they own it.

Well, I'm guessing that the ticklish relationship between a realistic, knowledgeable, experienced hairdresser and an idealistic, unrealistic, hardheaded client is somewhat similar, if complicated by the fact that the client is paying directly for the hairdresser's services, and therefore feels as if whatever the client demands should immediately be granted, without the slightest opposition. And yet, ostensibly, the hairdresser is the one who, like the professor, knows best. They know when a certain style will look absurd, they know when attempting this or that treatment will damage the hair. (They also know that if they give in to the insistent client, and the client subsequently leaves the shop baldheaded and furious, said client will tell everyone never to go to that shop—"Just look what they did to me!"—and they'll lose business.) It's a problem. *Look at him,* Michelle was likely thinking, *just look at him. There he sits, just got twisted last week, has no idea what he's talking about, and yet he's sitting in my chair telling me he doesn't want me to put wax on his locks. I wish he'd get a clue...* Oh, I had a pretty good idea what they were thinking, all right.

So they did what professors do, as a last resort, when confronted with a truculent, seemingly intractable, know-it-all student, however rare, in my experience, those students might be: they asserted their authority, their credibility; they demonstrated their knowledge base. They said, in effect: *We have experience. We know what we're doing. You, callow and painfully misinformed client, do not.* "The beeswax holds your hair together while it locks up," said Michelle patiently. "You want to get the locks to stay in place so they can be shampooed and not mesh back together." Nicole nodded soberly. Having said their piece, they waited for my response.

"Are you saying that unless you put something on the twists, then when I come in for a retwist, you won't be able to find the 'cuts' after you shampoo?" I used the same word B.J. had used when she worried aloud that I'd have this problem, only I turned it into a question instead of the statement B.J. had made.

"Exactly," said Michelle. "It'll just be hair; all together again. It's like you'd be starting all over again, just with freshly shampooed hair."

"I see," I said. And I did see. I saw why Michelle thought that it would "just be hair" again: It's likely only hairdressers with a "natural" dread philosophy ever become practiced at seeing the "cuts." It's not that the cuts aren't there, it's that you have to know how to find them, I thought. If B.J. can find them, then they can be found—it's not as if B.J. is some superhero with dread-ray vision. No, Michelle is used to maintaining locks her own way—and who can blame her, really? At the same moment I was saying "I see," however, I was wondering whether I'd be able to find a "natural" hair-care place somewhere in the Boston area, since Roots 'n Locks, it was clear, was not about "natural."

The War of Nature

I see dreadlocks the way Charles Darwin saw nature. Most people see dreads as hyper-natural, more natural even than the Afro, which was also called—hello—"the natural." *Just stop combing your hair*, millions of people believe, as I once believed, *and* voilà: *dreadlocks naturally appear*. Cue Darwin, from *On the Origin of Species*: "It is interesting to contemplate an entangled bank, clothed with many plants of many kinds, with birds singing on the bushes, with various insects flitting about, and with worms crawling through the damp earth...."

Such a natural scene is witnessed by millions of people daily, often with contented exhales and knowing smiles.

But Darwin didn't see nature in such a sentimental way:

> What a struggle between the several kinds of trees must here have gone on during long centuries, each annually scattering its seeds by the thousand; what war between insect and insect—between insects, snails, and other animals with birds and beasts of prey—all striving to increase, and all feeding on each other or on the trees or their seeds and seedlings, or on the other plants which first clothed the ground and thus checked the growth of trees!

Darwin understood that what might have looked placid and serene was a violent site for struggle: "each organic being...at some point of its life, during some season of the year, during each generation or at intervals, has to struggle for life, and to suffer great destruction." He calls this natural selection "the war of nature." Meaning, Yo, it may indeed be natural, but it sure ain't easy to achieve.

The dreadlocks everyone sees—and some of us want—take its own form of "war" and "struggle." Itching, scratching, the protection of twists against the ravages of sleep and the elements, the ongoing, persistent twisting of the hair, the uncertainty...oh, there's struggle, all right.

And it takes forever: "That natural selection will always act with extreme slowness, I fully admit," wrote Darwin, and am I the only one who hears a slight, exasperated "sigh" on the end of that sentence? "Nothing can be effected, unless favourable variations occur, and variation itself is apparently always a very slow process." It does "apparently" take, with locks *and* evolution, time for contested nature to take its course.

And hey, look: More than once, Darwin described the result of natural selection as "beautiful adaptations," after all. There might have been massive struggle, but what emerged were, he exults, "all those exquisite adaptations": lock after lock after dangling lock of the gorgeous results of that grand struggle.

But struggle it was, struggle it is, and struggle it will remain.

Slow, grand, and ongoing, dreadlocks are, indeed, a beautiful struggle—eventually evolving into a massive head of dread.

The Pure (iii)

In the end, I got a dry twist at Roots 'n Locks, nothing but water, but I left the shop troubled, with a much clearer sense of my dilemma. I also left the place with a far firmer understanding of B.J. When she talked about her philosophy a week earlier, I had no idea how exceptional she was. What I felt as I left Roots 'n Locks was akin to a child being introduced to Christianity and then going out and seeing just how cruel the world can be. B.J., I was discovering, was a hardcore evangelist for "natural" hair—the same kind of evangelist I am, among my composition students, for conversational prose. And it appeared that she was as isolated a voice in the wilderness of the black hair care world as I was in my approach to composition pedagogy. B.J.'s natural dread philosophy accounted for her zeal, her fire, her passion—all of which was infectious, and definitely made one want to become a part of her "natural" world. (I suspect that whatever success I might have had in converting composition students myself stemmed, in part, from my own passionate classroom presence.) If I hadn't gone to LA, I thought to myself, if I hadn't been steered to Twist and Shout, I'd be walking around Worcester with bigtime beeswax on my head, anxiously waiting to "lock up."

I slowly walked to my car shaking my head, wondering just what I was supposed to do about this problem. I grabbed a finger each time I ticked off my predicament: I've got a "natural" dread philosophy. I've got precious little knowledge. I've got no home. How do I find a place nearby that can give me what I need? I do have that DC connection, I remembered, but I've spent almost a hundred and fifty dollars on my fledgling locks already, and getting back and forth to DC with any regularity would be difficult, borderline impossible. Or do I just stick with Roots 'n Locks, instructing them on how to do my hair the way I did today? ("Water? That's all? You sure?" I could still hear their skeptical surprise at my so-called "instructions.") I could have them call B.J.—she told me before I left she'd have no problem with that—but it wasn't as if Nicole and Michelle sounded wide open to innovation, in any case. B.J.'s tough, but tough enough to override two experienced hair-care professionals who are used to doing things their way? I wouldn't think so. Nobody's that hardcore.

• • •

I was pissed. I berated myself all the way home, popped out of the car, and stomped into the house: I can't believe this. I can't *believe* this. The Pure. Again. Why do I always have to be the purist? Why? Why can't I—just once—do something the regular old way, whether it's good for me or not? For pete's sake, now I'm a *hair* purist? "'Natural' and only 'natural,' or I don't want any part of it"!? Please. I just want dreadlocks, okay? Do I have to set out on some sort of heroic quest? I mean, come *on*. I did get the stupid twists, didn't I? Wasn't that enough? I thought about how I used to be perfectly content reading both serious novels and pop trash. And for a long while now, almost as if I had no choice in the matter, all I want to read, all I value, is "literature"—and, increasingly, nonfictional, David Shieldsian "lyric" essays, at that. Then I thought about how, just days earlier, I was sitting streetside with Mark in Long Beach, arguing about insufferable smooth jazz, that nauseatingly odious jazz-fusion, was worthless, stinking crap. That if the music isn't based in the blues, if the musicians don't play with rhythmic attitude—better known as swing—then you can call it what you want, but you'd better not call it jazz. At one point Mark innocently asked, "Bert, why can't you listen to both?" Why? Because I just can't, that's why. In a perfect world I'd love to be able to listen to both. I'd love to be able to read both. But I just can't do it. I love the idea of cultural chaos; I love it down to my socks. I do. And the idea of being both a purist and an advocate of cultural chaos probably makes me sound like I'm insane. I'm a reluctant purist, but so what? Sometimes The Pure claims its own, kicking and screaming, personal will be damned. Does it have to claim me, now? Do I really have to be an iconoclast in the *type* of dreadlocks I get? Really? Aren't dreadlocks themselves iconoclastic enough?

"The Pure. The Pure." I stood in the foyer of my house, eyes shut tightly, fists to my forehead, spitting out the words in disgust. I backed into this one, for sure. I had no idea my sister was pointing me toward a "natural" black hair salon when she told me about Twist and Shout. But then, wasn't that me, sitting in Michelle's chair on the other side of the continent, dismissively declining to put hair junk on my twists, even though I first learned about the existence of "natural" dreadlocks exactly one week ago? I writhed in pain.

Ah, well, I thought, sighing loudly. I might as well ride it out. I'll call B.J. and tell her what they said, and she can advise me as to how to proceed. Another battle, I thought. That's just great. I really didn't ask for this, and I really don't need this, but here I am. My dukes are up; let's get down.

Against "Dredloc"

It's simple mathematics. Chicki-check it out:

Dreadlocks minus "a" equals dredlocks.

Dredlocks minus "k" equals dredlocs.

Dreads minus "a" equals dreds.

Locks minus "k" equals locs.

I set out to trace the lexical space between "dreadlocks" and "locs" to see what I'd find. What I discovered was: an agony. So much pain.... In the end, after my heart had been broken wide open, the math emerged with deadly clarity: Dreadlocks plus American slavery equals tragedy.

I was certainly aware that spelling the hairstyle "dredlocks" was widely seen by some blacks as more "positive" than spelling the hairstyle "dreadlocks." I knew such assertions were often accompanied by the saying, "There's nothing dreadful about my hair." It seems the spelling of "dread," when viewed through the "prison" of the positive/negative binary, just seems too *negative* for a hairstyle that just feels so *positive*. Solution? Snip that troublesome "a" and we're in business, right? Problem solved?

Not exactly. On a search for "dredlocks," Google quickly led me to this rather remarkable sentence, written the summer before the presidential election of 2008: "If we end up with a president whose child has dreds, as obama's does, I'm moving out of the fucking country (sic)." Aside from the fact that Malia Obama wore twists on her visit to London and not dreadlocks, this absurd sentence, all by itself, explodes any idea that the mere removal of an "a" can solve dreadlocks' positive-or-negative spelling issue. This person sounds pretty negative to me. (I'd be delighted to discover that the commenter followed through on his or her threat to leave the country upon Barack Obama's election, but somehow I doubt that exit ever occurred.) Still, let's give the person credit: That sentence did credibly and responsibly drain the problematic "a" from the word "dreads." So while the statement does, indeed, from a black perspective, seem fundamentally "negative," the *spelling* certainly appears "positive," yes?

But that's the tension I expected. I originally thought that spelling "dreadlocks" was all about positive versus negative, and nothing more. Sure, I realized that internalized oppression—understandable oppression, beaten into us over nearly 250 years of slavery plus 100 more years of legal second-class status—was at the root of such tension, but that fact seemed so abstract, so routine. The case of the subtractive "a"—the *dred*, not dre*a*d question—I saw as a coping mechanism. A creative, improvisational response to the "call" of American white supremacy. Altering the spelling to "dredlocks" and "locs" are a form, I thought, of black vernacular "play"; it's riffing, it's signifyin(g) on the original term—funnin' with words by a people who love improvisation, love repetition with a signal difference: Why simply spell it "dreadlocks" when you can snatch the "a" and smooth it out a little, y'know? Why just punch "locks" onto the page when you can clip the "k" and leave the remaining word streamlined and chill, the lexical equivalent of ace-deucing a ball cap up and to the side or backward, or intentionally sagging trousers past the buttocks—acknowledging standard usage and subverting it at the same time. Both "dredlock" and "loc" are phonetically safe; they sound the same—everyone knows what the speaker, what the writer is talking about—and yet there's room for play, for danger, for a twist, if you will. It's all good.

Enter slavery. Referring to the word "dreadlocks," Ayana D. Byrd and Lori L. Tharps, in *Hair Story: Untangling the Roots of Black Hair in America*, wrote this:

> The name derives from the days of the slave trade. When Africans emerged from the slave ships after months spent in conditions adverse to any personal hygiene, Whites would declare the matted hair that had grown out of their kinky unattended locks to be "dreadful." (For that reason, many today wearing the style chose to drop the *a* in *dreadlock* to remove all negative connotations.)

My heart broke when I read those words. It's nonsense, of course. For one, the length of the Middle Passage was rarely long enough for locking. While the passage time varied, slavers grew more efficient as the years of enslavement wore on. It could take as few as six weeks; extraordinarily rare was the six-month journey. But that's nothing. Byrd's and Tharps's scenario displays a huge, gulping lack of logic. Phrases like "When Africans emerged" and "Whites would declare" suggest that this episode occurred repeatedly, time and again, over and over, surely more than once. And yet, if that were the case, wouldn't there be some kind of documentary evidence of such repeated exchanges? Letters, journal entries, notes among merchants' financial books, ships' logs, newspaper articles, transcribed oral histories—*something*. But there's nothing. Not only that, but I've seen many, many documentary images of enslaved Africans—etchings, drawings, paintings, sketches, by eyewitness correspondents on both sides of the Atlantic—and few, if any, of the Africans have anything even remotely resembling dreadlocks. If the heads on the Africans in these countless images had contained dreadlocks, such correspondents would have been more than happy to represent them, perhaps thinking that dreadlocks would make them seem even more subhuman than was already presumed. But there were no dreadlocks. It never happened.

And yet, the dogged insistence of loxmen and -women everywhere to cleanse their lexical palates of that distasteful "a" persists. Isn't this the oddest place ever for Evelyn Higginbotham's "politics of respectability" to emerge, kicking and screaming? In *Righteous Discontent: The Women's Movement in the Black Baptist Church, 1880-1920*, Higginbotham argues that the politics of respectability was all about the "reform of individual behavior as a goal in itself and as a strategy for reform," and that such "uplift politics" actually included two audiences: black folk, who were encouraged to be respectable, and white folk, who needed to be shown that black folk could be respectable. Sound familiar? I would fully believe "there's nothing dreadful about my hair" as a solitary message from dread-wearers toward other black folk if there wasn't that nettlesome antebellum origin story that has whiteness at its core—and that leads me to believe this is, indeed, a respectability tale, and a sad one, at that.

It's as if black dread-wearers desperately needed to shove whiteness into the realm of black dread, since the true modern, Western origin of the style arrived with a name that just didn't seem quite respectable enough. It's almost like viewing the movie *Carrie* recast with dread blacks, and Carrie's mother's insistent chant to her daughter—"They're all gonna laugh at you, they're all gonna laugh at you"—was not actually moms, but was really the Dredloc Authority, with dread Carrie as the hapless, unconscious locks-wearer needing to be jerked back in line.

The ideological tension between these two stances—"dread" and "dred"—is absolutely fascinating to me. After all, the hairstyle itself is inherently oppositional, no matter how hard one might want to "tame" its push-back. Plus the idea that an oppositional hairstyle should need to be respectable, in any case, is odd and peculiar on its face. And then the idea that altering its *spelling* would somehow do the trick is even stranger still, since, phonetically and aurally, absolutely nothing has changed. I can almost imagine the most agitated of the spelling-changers responding to random comments on their locks with, "Oh, I've had them for a few years now. And I use the spelling d-r-e-d-l-o-c, by the way—'cause there's nothing dreadful about my hair." Really? Worse, I'll bet the most insistent, foot-stomping, fist-pounding-on-table of them might well respond to comments on his or her hair with a terse, preemptive, "How're you spelling that?" to their commenter. "Just want to make sure you understand that the spelling is d-r-e-d-l-o-c, y'know." Seriously? Any step toward "dredloc" is a step away from the deliciously complicated cultural chaos of "dreadlock"—although, of course, the introduction of "dredloc" into the mix does contribute to the inherently chaotic study of the style.

My own stance is clear and unambiguous: The spelling is d-r-e-a-d-l-o-c-k (I am a purist, after all). And anyway, I remain a virulent pun supremacist; always have been, always will be: "Dread" serves a double meaning, initially for the Rastafarians, and still, somewhat, today, signaling a specific hairstyle as well as some grudging form of outsider status. I insist on pronouncing that doubled status—literally.

The best essay on the subject is "Slave Hair and African American Culture in the Eighteenth and Nineteenth Centuries," published in the *Journal of Southern History* in 1995 by Shane White and Graham White, professors at the University of Sydney (the essay was later included in their acclaimed book *Stylin': African-American Expressive Culture, from Its Beginnings to the Zoot Suit*). The authors painstakingly combed through actual historical documents, including page after page of newspaper advertisements for runaway slaves. Perhaps it turns out to be the best essay on the subject due to what's not in it: At no point did they stumble upon any such reference to Byrd's and Tharps's account of the naming of dreadlocks. I know this because I emailed Professor Shane White and asked him myself. He seemed surprised to discover that any such origin-of-"dreadlocks" tale existed: "I've never even seen those sorts of stories in print, actually, let alone seen any suggestion that there is the slightest bit of truth in them," he replied.

But then he said something that echoed what I'd been morosely pondering since I first confronted the issue of the spelling of "dreadlocks"—or the issue of using the term "dreadlocks" at all. When he said it, it turned the Spelling-Dreadlocks Question from really weird to ultimately tragic. Shane White, in just 21 words, broke what remained of the little bit of heart I had left: "I am afraid the material says rather more about the authors and the making up of a mythology than anything else."

And there it was. The Rastafarians named the hairstyle. Yes, it has been a hairstyle since long before Ras Tafari was born, but still: "Dreadlocks," the word, came from the Rastafarians. Period. The confusion, the ongoing clashing and blurring of the style, the uncertainty of the origins of the style, the radically divergent meanings of the style, all remain deeply attractive and compelling to me—most of the time. But this...This was, to my eyes, incontrovertible evidence of the ongoing tragedy of American slavery, evidence of a people still in recovery, still traumatized from 350 years of physical, then legal bondage. The eagerness, online and elsewhere, to believe the unbelievable—the willingness to accept the preposterously unacceptable—is the product of hundreds of years of psychic pain, and the pain is right there on the surface. It's palpable. Inventing an oppressive mythology from which the name "dreadlocks" emerged is, indeed, the coping strategy I always thought it was. For all my interrogation of and ultimate dismissal of "dredloc," in the end my own sympathetic understanding of the reality of all those years of white oppression—oppression that continues today—means that, from my point of view, I see the imagining of the "slave-ship/dreadful" scenario in the first place, and then the widespread, subsequent, unconscionable, knee-jerk *belief* in the scenario as, at least in part, an attempt to deal with the ongoing legacy of American slavery.

It's painful to acknowledge. It hurts.

They Can't Stop Me (i)

My foolish, head-rubbing lapse cost me a visit to Roots 'n Locks and $50, but it was worth it. I didn't want a Bad Hair Day the morning of an important interview and, in the end, I didn't. My hair looked exactly the way I wanted it to look. And the interview was successful: I would be teaching at Brown that fall as a visiting professor. Wearing dreadlocks at hip, multi-culti Brown, though, would not quite be the same as being dread at the College of the Holy Cross. Getting twisted in LA was, I knew, both symbolically and literally, going about as far from Holy Cross as I could get. Now that I was back in Worcester, I wondered about on-campus reaction to my hair. Even though I was officially on research leave in the fall, I'd still be on campus now and then.

Stakes were fairly high, too. I hate to admit that I did consider the tenure ramifications of going dread. It would be wonderful if I could honestly say I never gave it a thought. But I can't say that. I can say, however, that for once I didn't think about it long and hard. Everybody confronts a behavioral line somewhere deep inside themselves. Every day we all make certain concessions to the fact that we're living in a society among certain norms and realities. *Les enfants terribles* among us delight in pushing that internal line out as far as possible. Other people meekly toe whatever line is etched for them. I believe most people struggle, either consciously or unconsciously, with being either too conciliatory or not conciliatory enough. My own line, I quickly decided, was my hairline. I knew it was a calculated risk, but I also knew that I was going to come up for tenure in three years one way or another, and the me that got approved or unapproved—the me I wanted to get evaluated—was absolutely going to be wearing dreadlocks. Sure, I could have waited until after the tenure decision to get twisted, that would have been safest, but I didn't want safety—I expressly wanted to avoid safety. I wanted to mix danger and rebellion into my good-guy demeanor, dammit, and what better way to do that than to place tenure—essentially a guaranteed job for life—in the balance.

I would just have to see how the whole thing played out during my periodic visits to campus while on leave and when I came back in the spring. No, I didn't wrestle with this one. No tortured consideration, no dread-or-not-to-dread fluctuation. It's my hair, I decided, and I'll do with it what I please. Nobody can stop me.

Five Charged, On-Screen Seconds

1986

Imagine being able to tell how a city, if not an entire region, feels about dreadlocks while watching a film in which no one wears dreadlocks! I return, once again and always, to Spike Lee's *She's Gotta Have It.* Joie Lee, Spike's sister, plays Nola Darling's ex-roommate, and when we first see her on-screen her back is to the camera as she sits at a sewing machine. For several seconds all we hear is the whir of the machine as we watch her head, arms, and shoulders move as she sews. Finally, she stops and begins to turn around. The screen goes to black and we see her character's name, "Clorinda Bradford," in white letters at the bottom of the black screen. Then she has her close-up: Her luminous eyes and beautiful, expressive face silently fill the screen. Although she sighs once, for five full seconds she says nothing. Then she begins to speak. It's a short scene, and it doesn't really stand out much at all. A minor character introduced. Big deal.

Offscreen, though, the scene actually was a big deal, at least for me. I first saw the film in Manhattan, while it was still in early, limited release. (A then-still-unknown Spike Lee was hawking T-shirts on the sidewalk in front of the theater.) As that scene unspooled and flickered up onto the screen,

I was sitting among mostly black, hip, New York sophisticates. When Joie Lee faced the camera as Clorinda Bradford, taking a break from sewing to speak directly to us, we audience members simply waited for her to speak. We gazed up at her hair, a style called—well, actually, if it has a name I'm unaware of it. Whatever it's called, it's much more common nowadays than it was in 1986. At first glance it seems massively uncombed, just wildly *out there*; it's hair that looks as if the smoke just recently stopped floating off of it, the result of electric shock. At second or third glance, however, it's clear that the hair is styled to look the way it does. There's an intentional symmetry to such styles that announce them *as* styles. For a long five seconds we stared at her as she stared into the camera, staring back at us, and when she finally spoke, we listened to what she said and the film moved on.

But when I went to a Broad Street theater to see the film again in Richmond, later that same summer, that same scene was magically transformed. Oh, the scene played out the same on-screen, of course. But in Richmond, when Joie Lee turned around from having her back to the camera, the screen went black, and then the same beautiful head appeared. But this time she wasn't looking out at an audience of cosmopolitan New Yorkers, she was looking out at an all-black Virginia audience, and those people *screamed* at the sight of her. The Richmond audience filled in that five-second filmic space by laughing at Joie Lee and her hair. There was nothing subtle about it. It felt like nasty, denigrating, mean-spirited laughter. And what made it all the more surreal was how spontaneous the laughter was. There was such unanimity in the response, such instantaneous cohesion. *Everybody* in that theater howled with what I heard as derisive, sneering laughter. (I actually wondered, for a moment or two, whether the audience presumed Spike had intentionally had his sister's hair styled that way for comedic purposes.) It was my first real introduction to the depth of regional differences when it comes to black hair.

In some ways, though, these two radically different reactions to the same wild haircut made sense. Spike not only included that extremely intimate, this-feels-"better-than-bonin'" scene when Nola Darling scratched and greased Mars Blackmon's head in *She's Gotta Have It*, but his student film at NYU was called *Joe's Bed-Stuy Barbershop: We Cut Heads*. And *School Daze*, his follow-up to *She's Gotta Have It*, featured a musical number called "Straight and Nappy." It's no surprise, then, that the end credits for *She's Gotta Have It* close with this odd and telling assertion: "**THIS FILM HAS NO DRUGS AND NO JHERI-CURLS**" (the line of credit is underlined, bolded, *and* capitalized for triple emphasis). It's clear that black hair has deep meaning for Spike Lee. And yet, no dreadlocks appear in the film—unless we count Joie Lee's unconventional hairstyle as proxy. I'm not saying she was wearing dreadlocks—she wasn't. But she was wearing a hairstyle that was every bit as provocative as dreadlocks might have been to that black Richmond audience in the summer of 1986. *Laugh at it. Reduce it. Control it.* That scene showed me that the *idea* of messy, wildly uncontrollable black hair was right there in the theater that night, even if dreadlocks weren't actually on-screen.

Laugh at It. Reduce It. Control It. (ii)

1988

Watching a black male comedian on cable television as he refers to Tracy Chapman and her single "Fast Car," from her self-titled album. The sole image on the cover of the disc is a pensive, dreadlocked Chapman, about whom the comedian scoffs and says, "Looks like she's been holding her head outside of a fast car."

I might have laughed. It is kind of funny. Whether I laughed or not, I do remember being struck by the fact that the joke was being told at all. The joke suggests that the comedian thought that dreadlocks' cultural and visual *difference* would resonate with his (multiracial) audience, and the laughter he received suggested he was right. As with any joke, listeners must be familiar with the context of the joke in order to "get" it—let alone find it funny—and this joke's premise was Chapman's comparatively wild and crazy locks. With the sheer volume of African Americans who now wear their hair in dreadlocks, it's hard to imagine anyone telling that joke today, but it does show how provocative dread was during its golden age.

Going Outside (v)

1989

There is no essay more important to me than "The New Black Aesthetic," by Trey Ellis. In this essay, published in 1989, Ellis talks knowingly and enthusiastically about "cultural mulattos" (such as Tracy Chapman, actually), post-integration black kids who, like me, grew up walking on the high, thin fence between white and black culture and who, like me, figured out how to step and move, how to dance on that narrow fence instead of walking gingerly, afraid of falling into one world or the other. "Spike Lee, Fishbone, and I," Ellis writes at one point, "along with the battalions of other young black artists I run into more and more frequently, all grew up feeling misunderstood by both the black worlds and the white. Alienated (junior) intellectuals, we are the more and more young blacks getting back into jazz and the blues; the only ones you see at punk concerts; the ones in the bookstore wearing little, round glasses and short, neat dreads; some of the only blacks who admit liking both Jim and Toni Morrison."

Later in the essay, he repeats his contention that "Most all young, black intellectuals" wear "little, round glasses, Ghanaian, kente-cloth scarves, and, increasingly, tiny, neat dreadlocks." Ellis adds, parenthetically, "Unfortunately, my hair is still too short for dreads," before stating, "Still, I am proud of my also-stylish 'Fade' or 'jar-head' cut, only one-curl high on the sides of my head—so short you can see the scalp." Ellis never did get dreadlocks, but obviously the style was a presence on his cultural radar screen by the late 80s.

He was, it's clear, wearing his own dread-goggles in the years he surveyed our age cohort, and by the time he was ready to write "The New Black Aesthetic" he had come up with a stylistic, mathematical equation: *Little, round glasses* plus *short, neat dreadlocks* equals *young, black intellectual.* I have to wonder if the reason he saw his generation of young black intellectuals with "tiny" dreadlocks is because those fringe blacks who were attracted to the style all got twisted at more or less the same time. Locks grow—far too slowly, but they do grow—and it appears that as Trey Ellis walked around New York and Los Angeles in the 1980s he was witnessing the (literal) growth of the golden age of dreadlocks. I wonder, had Ellis written his essay a few years later, if he would not have referred to how short all those dreads were, because they wouldn't have been so short by then. There's no question he was seeing a *lot* of black heads with dreads, and it's fascinating and telling to me that so many of the locks he saw were short—meaning new—and that they were "neat"—meaning they were being carefully nursed along by a knowing locktician. I believe this was the signal moment—Ellis wrote the essay between 1983 and 1987—that a critical mass of blacks adopted the style, and that these style-forward dreadlock wearers combined with Whoopi Goldberg's mainstream media presence to make dreadlocks a widespread hairstyle in the 1990s.

It's not surprising that hair played an important role in the visual Ellis used for the black intellectuals who launched the post-black era. It's striking, though, that *neatness* seems to Americanize these intellectuals' dreadlocks, effectively separating them from reggae, Rasta, and Jamaica—particularly from the sense of these intellectuals' locks being uncontrollably, wildly Rasta-natural. Add a stick, then, and widen the triangle to make it the Essential Dreadlock Square—crime-point, clown-point, heritage-point… and *boho*-point (although those last two might overlap at times)—"boho" meaning, of course, bohemian.

• • •

I read about bohemia. I dream about bohemia. I'm enchanted by bohemia.

I am *so* not bohemian.

There's a yellow manila envelope in my file cabinet with "The Corporate Shuffle… 1985–1988" scrawled on the front. I don't even have to open it. I know what's inside. I was working at a market research firm in Richmond, Virginia, after I left radio, before I went back to school. I wore a short, neat haircut, and I often wore my corporate uniform, and wore it with pride: khaki pants, loafers, button-down Oxford shirt, yellow, red, or blue power tie, blue blazer with gold buttons. I wore that uniform on and off the corporate snide. Brown robot.

• • •

I must stare down my sordid past with shoulders squared; I must ask the searing question, no matter the wince-inducing answer: *What was I doing in 1986? Where was I in 1988? What did my hair look like in 1992?* Dread's golden age came and went, from 1979 or so to the early 1990s: *What did you do during the war, Daddy?* I grew up in suburbia, kid. I've always lived in suburbia—and I don't just mean my body. I was 27 years old in 1986. I cared enough about black art to make a special trip to New York to see *She's Gotta Have It* after I read about it in the *Village Voice*, and I instantly fell deeply in love, not just with the film but with the Brooklyn lives the characters lived on-screen. Artist Nola Darling. Model/actor Greer Childs. Hip-hop scofflaw Mars Blackmon. Even goofy Jamie Overstreet. Did I ever actually imagine, even for one second, moving to New York and becoming them, versions of them? No, I did not.

I was 29 years old in 1988. I read Trey Ellis's "The New Black Aesthetic" and was entranced with the vivid, electric reality of viable, lively, oppositional post-60s black art—and the artists who made it, the bohos who consumed it, the intellectuals who explained it. I read, reread, and re-reread that essay—I could probably, even now, recite portions of it by heart. Jerome Benton couldn't find a bigger mirror to hold up onstage for Morris Day than I felt "The New Black Aesthetic" held up a mirror for me—well, the me, anyway, I imagined my interior self to be. Did newly married Bert Ashe ever think, even fleetingly, of fleeing Virginia and moving to Brooklyn, growing dreadlocks, and invading the New York art scene? No, he did not.

I was 33 years old in 1992. I did not have dreadlocks. I had a short, dreadfully conventional haircut. I luxuriated in the splashy wealth of black-directed films that poured onto American screens in 1991 and 1992. I danced with bohemia, sure. But it wasn't the foxtrot or the tango or the cha-cha-cha, it was slam dancing—that jarring, struggle-to-keep-your-feet type of dance, or it was post-50s, two-people-at-a-distance dancing, which inevitably includes moments when your dance partner turns her back on you. That was it; that was my stiff-legged, ongoing dance with bohemia. Could growing dreadlocks possibly illuminate in some small way the tiny, ember-like boho-longing that always lingered deep within my psychic woodpile? I hoped so.

The post-soul aesthetic refers to one who is born or came of age after the civil rights movement, and I was that one. Slouching in the seats of the playhouse and the movie house, pausing before art on gallery walls, shoving in the mosh pit of the club, patting my foot and nodding my head in the seats of the jazz club—I watched, I viewed, I listened, I heard. I danced. I danced with bohemia. I was a spectator, an audience member, and my clothing, my hair, reflected my suburban status. That was the only way I knew how to do it. From a distance.

Going Outside (vi)

The magnetic tug of suburbia was too strong; I couldn't summon enough escape velocity to transcend it. I hate that cheesy saying, "Anywhere you go, there you are"—but it's true: Reinvention is overrated. Identity is not substitutive. Identity is additive.

And anyway, passing for bohemian might just be more fun than actually being bohemian. I went to a rock club called the Nanci Raygun one night some years back, down on then-gritty Grace Street here in Richmond. Some VCU kids, during fashion week, were screening *Afro-Punk* (original title: *Afro-Punk: The "Rock 'n' Roll Nigger" Experience*). Richmond's black punk-rock community was out and down. I'd never been to the Raygun before, and I didn't get back to it before it closed, but that night the club was a bizarre fusion of cozy and homey, what with a table of cookies and brownies and the cheery welcoming vibe of those hosting the screening, combined with the rough, grungy club interior and the aggressive styles—spiky hair, tattoos, torn black clothing, studs and piercings—worn by the attendees. The tension between open-as-a-warm-hug and tough-as-a-punch-to-the-face was intoxicating.

Before the film started I sat at the bar, had a beer, chatted with a black guy who looked exactly like novelist Paul Beatty—this guy was even named "Paul"—and a white guy who was attending Mary Washington College. I have no idea what they thought of me, of why I was there, of what I represented. Before long the young black punk who had organized the screening stood up to introduce the film, and she became increasingly emotional as she talked about the depths of what the film meant to her. I stood in the middle of the audience, black punks and white punks to my left and to my right, and black punks on-screen talking about the black punk experience, and I loved being there, loved that I was viewing the film for the first time exactly the way I should be viewing it: subject matter, text, context, all in sync, everything perfect.

But if I'd been trying to be bohemian—instead of being conscious of having earlier kissed my wife's cheek and tousled my kids' hair, closed the door of my Colonial house in my "Ashley Grove" subdivision, walked to my Toyota Camry sitting in my Chesterfield County driveway, rolled through suburban streets until I got into the city, parked and walked into the club, knowing full well that I was floating into a bohemian space and bathing myself with a bohemian experience but that I wasn't getting wet, I don't know that I'd've enjoyed it as much. I was not bohemian. If I'd contorted myself to be bohemian, I would have had to monitor my guise—and it absolutely would have been a guise. Instead, I just tried to be as unself-conscious as possible, although I couldn't help wondering if my dreadlocks mediated my suburbanity and this momentary, one-time-only punk experience. Was I a poseur? I didn't feel like one. I don't think I looked like one. I know I wasn't acting like one. And yet, as I stood there, screened on every side, my hair, my body, my being, ensconced in, surrounded by, immersed in punk—while being, myself, decidedly not punk—I did wonder, at last, how a novelist or a cultural critic or an anthropologist would describe me.

Fuzzy Phase (ii)

I dropped by Roots 'n Locks in mid-August to chat with Michelle and Nicole about my hair. It was crazy fuzzy by then. The thing is, I was determined to go another two weeks before I did anything to it. That would take me four days past the month B.J. told me to wait before shampooing my hair, and I was thinking seriously (although whether I could actually pull it off is another question) about not getting shampooed at all at my monthly appointment.

We talked. As Michelle and Nicole stood behind the heads they were working on, I paced back and forth in front of their chairs, slowly increasing my knowledge base. Here's what I found out: Dread wannabes put all sorts of silliness in their hair in order to get it to lock up faster. Beeswax is just the beginning. Lemon juice, as B.J. mentioned, is also a favorite. (I said to Nicole, "Did you ever really put lemon juice in someone's hair?" She casually, wordlessly leaned back, stretched her hand to the row of containers on the counter nearest her, and held up a bottle for me to see.) And eggs. Yes. Eggs. I tried to imagine walking around with eggs and lemon juice twisted into my hair, and I couldn't do it. I guess I just didn't have that active an imagination.

The more they talked, the more I heard that people who enter the Lemon and Egg Zone do so for two reasons. The primary reason is they want dreads and they want them yesterday. The accent is on speed. The secondary reason is that they're simply trying to hold their locks together when they shampoo, so they won't have to start over again, as Michelle had said. Now, that second reason was certainly something I could understand. But can't I get it done this way? I wondered. All I want are legitimate locks that look good to me. Is that too much to ask?

Meanwhile, I was bleeding locks-related money. Just gushing. I had no idea getting dreadlocks would cost so much. Roots 'n Locks was going to charge me somewhere in the neighborhood of $50 every time I got touched-up. I was reminded of the time I assigned a paper and told the class that the required length was "somewhere in the neighborhood" of ten to twelve pages. This kid raises his hand and asks if it's okay if his paper resides "a few blocks closer to nine." Well, I sure wished those touch-ups lived a few blocks closer to $25, since I had to get my locks "touched" twice a month—the irony being that I was trying so hard not to touch them myself!

I tried to look at the expense this way: Since I'd been cutting my own hair for well over ten years, I had been saving 20 or 30 dollars a month, maybe more, and saving time, as well. Now, after not having spent any money at all on my hair for years, I'd decided on a hairstyle that might look low maintenance, but actually is extremely high maintenance. So I swallowed hard and committed. I would be going to get my hair touched-up just about every two weeks. "Any fewer than that," Nicole told me, teaching me something else, "and your locks might break off. The hair closer to your head isn't as strong as the hair that's dangling."

I mentioned the cost issue to Val that evening, just before she went upstairs, and she scoffed. As we stood at the bottom of the stairs she reminded me of how, in the years before she cut her hair, I used to tell her nonchalantly that she needed to get her hair done, even though I had no idea what it cost. When I told her I'd have to get twisted every two weeks, she was surprised that I wanted such frequent hands-on maintenance.

"Well, you've got to 'control' them, Val," I responded, employing a term Nicole had used earlier in the day. "That is, if you want them to look right."

"Oh, I get it," Val said breezily before she continued up the stairs. "You don't want real dreadlocks. You want pseudo dreads."

Pseudo dreads. It was as if I was suddenly up on the landing next to Val, watching myself standing uncomfortably at the bottom of the stairs, the frown on my face suggesting that the words "pseudo" and "dreads" were bouncing off each other inside my head like Lotto balls inside that spinning, see-through globe, just before the drawing.

I decided, after a moment or two, that I didn't like the term at all.

• • •

Later that evening Val and I and the kids watched an unbelievably cheesy documentary called *400 Years Without A Comb*. At one point, the filmmakers carefully and consciously portrayed a young enslaved family as each having shoulder-length dreadlocks. I thought the mother's locks looked great. And the father's dreads were roots-looking locks, very long, thick, and unruly. Again, they looked fine, if that was his preference. But the portrayal of the dread children was most fascinating. At one point a grandmotherly woman yanked one of the children's dreadlocks and barked to his mother, "Can't you do anything with this child's hair? Don't you have a comb?"

It was unreal. For one thing, again, with the possible exception of somebody like Topsy in *Uncle Tom's Cabin*, I've never had the impression that antebellum blacks, fictional or otherwise, wore dreadlocks—if, indeed, even Topsy had. Photos of freedmen, of sharecroppers and the like, all showed them with short to medium-length naturals. Yes, their hair looked thick and tough to manage, but no, it definitely wasn't locked.

For another: Dreadlocks is a contemporary hairstyle! To superimpose a contemporary hairstyle onto the heads of enslaved African Americans was a curious gesture, to say the least. Now, the video was produced in 1989, during the golden age, but I saw dreadlocks being used to mark these characters as hyper-black. Very strange viewing.

"So, Val," I said, watching the screen as the tangled and matted and obviously non-beauty-parlored dreadlocks of that little boy were getting jerked around by his on-screen grandma, "Are those 'pseudo dreads'?"

She just smiled her enigmatic smile.

Border Patrol (ii)

I love it when boundaries move so slowly no one can tell. Words are like that. They're always on the move, slowly losing one meaning while gradually gaining another. "Awful" once meant full-of-awe. "Like," as spoken punctuation, began as hip slang for 1940s black bebop musicians and post-war hipsters; by the 1980s, having travelled through the Beat Generation in the 1950s, it had somehow arrived as the word of choice—often several times a sentence—for white suburban teens. Words like "irregardless," "conversate," words rejected as crude errors, may one day take their place in common usage, and no one alive will remember the struggle to keep them out of popular parlance. "Literally" means actually, as in reality. But as more and more people blithely use "literally" as emphasis, when they truly mean "figuratively," "literally" will eventually and completely mean "figuratively." As John McWhorter once wrote, "we are safest thinking of any word's current signification as temporary." The definitional line is moving; we're in the midst of the transition, even if we can't see it, even if we can see it and can't stand it. Hair is like that. We can't see the progression, we can't observe the daily movement. But hair grows, and the difference between one row of twists and another gets obscured daily. Rude twisting enforces separation; still, the spies, the scouts, the slim insurgent strands of hair smear and fuzz and smudge locked lines. Locked boundaries blur. Slowly. Incessantly.

The Pure (iv)

Question: How are dreadlocks sometimes like a mullet?
Answer: A brother who insists on having a sharp "cut" line framing his temple and sideburns, with dreadlocks otherwise spilling out of his head, does, indeed, have the dread version of a mullet: Call it…the drullet.

The mullet is often derided as "business in front, party in the back." But it's ultimately derided, I believe, for one simple reason: It's too obvious. The beautiful thing about dreadlocks is that even with all the conflicting messages and blurring boundaries and signifying oppositions constantly cross-firing inside the style itself, most viewers have no idea of this. They see dreadlocks, the locks register in their heads, but the style means so many different things to so many different people that a person wearing the style in public prompts countless different thought-bubbles hovering above the heads of those silent public observers.

I love that about dreadlocks. The style is right out there, making a vivid statement. Regardless of what that statement might mean to the wearer or the viewer or the combination of both. And yet, the reason the mullet is considered such a fashion risk is because the wearer won't commit: The dude wants it both ways. He wants to be officious and neat, adapting to contemporary facial convention, and at the same time he wants to enjoy the cultural subversion of long male hair. America has turned thumbs-down on the mullet in the same way any other namby-pamby fence-sitter gets the American diss, and for me it breaks down with Funkadelican simplicity: If you ain't gonna get it on? Then "Take Your Dead Ass Home!"

As much as I love dreadlocks, I love just as much the rank indeterminacy of dreadlocks. That's why I tremble under the weight of The Pure; that's why I still feel queasy about the way The Pure dominates my thinking on dreadlocks—and just about everything else. But what to do? Aesthetic preferences are what they are—there's simply no accounting for taste. We can try to influence our aesthetic preferences, we can even feel bad about having them, but in the end, alas, there is, finally, this: I just don't like the drullet. In fact, I hate it. To get twisted, to go through the locking process, to end up dread is to enter and move through an experiential tube, a passageway, one where, once the twistee emerges on the other side of that tube, all the worries and concerns about neatness and "correctness" should matter just a little bit less. Dreadlocks are about the delightful blur, about the joyous smearing of precise head-grooming. Sporting a clean edge while wearing dreadlocks feels fraudulent to me. Wearing dreadlocks with a carved line is like a black Baptist churchgoer attending Sunday service in tank top and flip-flops, like a musician playing straight-ahead jazz with an electric bass. Commit. *Commit.* I just can't bring myself to see it any other way. Give in to the fuzzy; learn to love it or, at least, live with it; or, at last, learn that you might well need to cut the dreadlocks off.

—I am The Pure and I approved this message—

• • •

In the end, I called B.J., my esteemed locktician. I was still troubled by my dread dilemma. She didn't seem surprised at all by the recent developments. She did, after all, pretty much predict it. B.J. advised me to get my hair shampooed, but not vigorously, no rubbing or scraping. All told, she wanted me to do three things:

One: Get Val to retwist the new growth. "Take some water, and comb through the area that's been twisted. That," she said, "will clean the hair as she's doing it."

Two: After a couple of days, very carefully shampoo the twists, with a minimum of shampoo and a maximum of effort to keep the "cuts" in place. I told her Val had suggested wearing a hair net. "Not a bad idea," B.J. said.

Three: Go in and get a retwist from Roots 'n Locks, the local place. Then I'd be on track; the locking process would continue apace.

They'd look decent, if not "pseudo," in the interim, even though the new growth would make its presence felt. I hung up after I bade B.J. good-bye. It did feel good to tell B.J. that I hadn't let Nicole or Michelle put beeswax or any other chemical in my hair. "They know that's not going to happen," I'd said to B.J. I tried not to sound too proud of myself.

They Can't Stop Me (ii)

Sitting at the kitchen table, listening to Val relate the sober conversation she'd had with Jordan in the locker room at Assumption College after the kids' first swimming lesson:

> "Why does Daddy have dreadlocks?"
> "Because he wants them. He likes how they look."
> "Will he always have them?"
> "For as long as he wants them. Why?"
> [Long pause]
> "I want the old Daddy back..."

Dread Lit Syllabus (iv)

Scooping her up in its claw, the cyborg stares at her quizzically, the light in its eyes softening with what appears to be affection. Its jaw snaps open.

Bubbles is tossed inside. Crunch!

INT. Cyborg—the Image Chamber.

Negromancer

Screaming at the top of her lungs, Bubbles tumbles through the tunnels of the cyborg's twisted plumbing and lands on the octagonal floor of a black-lit room with a pastiche of ever changing imagery on its walls. She sits up and stares in confusion.

As her eyes adjust to the ultraviolet light, she sees a blurred, backlit Silhouette shuffle from the image chamber's walls. An empty white linen SUIT slowly walks into focus. The suit's pant legs jerk like a marionette's and a pair of white gloves hovers below its sleeves. Lavender-colored vapors swell from the opening in the neck of its shirt collar and condense into a floating mass of glow-in-the-dark dreads. Two luminous eyes and a plump, red mouth glow in the ovoid space under the nest of knotted hair.

—Darius James, *Negrophobia*, 1992

Inscrutability (ii)

Greeting my friend Lindsay, after he arrived at a roadside fast-food restaurant in Delaware to drive me to his house in Washington, DC, my beloved Honda having just been totaled in that four-car accident on I-95…

> "You always said you were going to do that," he said, knowingly shaking his head as he shook my hand.

(Now, I don't recall any specific moment when I told him I would get dreadlocks, but clearly I must have. My twists seemed to be some sort of litmus test: How well did a given person know me? If they didn't know me at all, like at Brown, they'd have never seen me any other way. If they only knew me a bit, then maybe they'd be surprised at the hair move. Apparently, though, if they knew me well, the dreads were more confirmation than innovation. Val certainly knew where I was headed. So did Niecy. So did my mother. And Linz, as well, seemed not the slightest bit surprised.)

• • •

Pausing for a moment on the steps of Sullivan Hall at Worcester State College as a friend, the director of Worcester's Charles Houston Cultural Project, walks up…

"Aha," she said brightly, "you're doing the Rastafarian thing!"

Death Sentence (iii)

1990

Every golden age needs a statement movie. I would have preferred a complicated, disturbing, preferably dark, dreadlocks-laden film with a statement that was as provocative as the style—but we're left with...*Marked for Death.* Of all mainstream Hollywood movies, *Marked for Death* likely stands as the one American-made film with more dreaded heads in it than any other. Given that likelihood, I'm pretty sure I hear the title differently than the way the movie's producers expect. It's a Steven Seagal movie, and the title is consistent with his other films: *Hard to Kill, Above the Law, Out for Justice*...you get the idea. I'm sure we're supposed to understand that it's the Steven Seagal character who's "marked for death," but I can't help feeling that, by 1990, after more than a decade of dire warnings about Jamaican drug posses, the MOVE imbroglio, and America's general suspicion of stylistic dissenters, it's the dreadlock-wearing innocent bystanders in the fictional world of the movie who're *marked for death.* Seagal's the hero; he ain't got nothing to worry about...

The movie is stuffed with violent, dreadlocked Jamaicans, and it screened, at its widest release, in nearly 2,000 theaters in the United States, ultimately grossing $57,968,936 worldwide. The plot revolves around a so-called Jamaican drug posse led by Screwface, creepy-eyed and dreadlocked, who invade a placid Northeastern town. Even though *60 Minutes* had introduced Americans to scary, automatic-weapons-toting, drug-addled "Rastafarians" years earlier, the point of the film is that Americans, even small-town Americans, need to be on guard, because the Jamaicans are coming! The Jamaicans are coming! Here's a key moment from the screenplay that occurs early in the film:

> *Like Los Angeles, New York, and Washington, small-town America now has blood in its streets, as a gang shoot-out in*

> *Lincoln Heights tonight has left four dead. Although less than one percent of Jamaican immigrants are involved, Jamaican gangs, known as "posses," are now dominating the American drug trade, with more than ten thousand members trafficking drugs in twenty states. According to justice department officials, they are as disciplined as they are violent. Torture and maiming are posse trademarks, and posse gunman are said to prefer shooting their victims in public. Sources estimate they have committed 1400 murders in three and a half years.*
>
> —Dale Harimoto, WXTV, Chicago

Forty-four seconds of "news," and it's probably unclear to the movie audience whether this is "real" information or script dialogue or somehow both. In fact, it's an odd combination of a factual-seeming context for a fictional text. This is not a documentary—it's a major motion picture, produced by Hollywood. But to heighten the realism, the film's producers cast a real news reporter, who's using her real name, although she reports fake news for a television station that doesn't exist. This breathless, urgent reporter, standing before rotating, blue-and-red squad-car lights, appears to be doing a stand-up on location at a true crime scene—or, seemingly, easily could be, if this were real life. Harimoto's strident reporting does suggest that the troublesome portion of Jamaican immigrants is minor relative to the overall number ("less than one percent of Jamaican immigrants are involved"), but then quickly implies that said minor portion seems so overwhelmingly violent and disruptive ("they are as disciplined as they are violent. Torture and maiming are posse trademarks, and posse gunman are said to prefer shooting their victims in public") that making any real distinctions between them and the majority of Jamaican immigrants is useless—better to distrust them all.

The bad guys are "Rastafarians"; they all wear dreadlocks. Scenes of pseudo voodoo imagery float throughout the flimsy plot. The message this film leaves is blindingly clear: If you see someone wearing dreadlocks, beware. Vestiges of that message linger into the present day, years after the golden age. I was checking in at the ticket counter at Los Angeles International Airport the year I got twisted, heading back to Massachusetts, when the woman on the other side of the counter pleasantly informed me that I was one of the "randomly selected" passengers who'd have to get their luggage x-rayed. I shrugged, lugged my bag a hundred or so feet to my right, got the bag x-rayed, hugged my father goodbye, and got on the flight.

It wasn't until later that Val told me that my father believed I had been singled out because of my hair. And maybe I was. It was entirely possible that the woman behind the counter stared at my tangled head and saw: suspect. (If so, she was a fantastic actress. I possess sensitive antennae for white discomfort with black presence, just like any other adult black person, and my antennae picked up absolutely no "funny vibe" from her whatsoever. If not for my father's reading of the situation, I would never have given it another thought.) In my father's opinion—an opinion I don't disagree with, either—a "bull's-eye" was gradually twisting out of my head. He thought my hair would have me standing in harm's way—*Marked for Death*—arms crossed, my silhouette in Public Enemy crosshairs. *And he could be right*, I thought. *He's probably right. He is right.*

Laugh at It. Reduce It. Control It. (iii)

1990-1991

In an episode from the fourth season of the TV show A Different World, *Colonel Taylor gets upset with Dwayne Wayne, because Wayne has been tutoring the colonel's son in math, but hasn't been getting through. In the episode called "Tales from the Exam Zone," an outraged Colonel Taylor heatedly insists to Dwayne Wayne,*

"My son knows as much about math as a Rastafarian knows about Dippity-do!"

• • •

Like clockwork—as if it's a culturally scripted inevitability—America insists, once again, on balancing the disturbing, dreadlocks-equals-Scary-Negroes narrative with the all-too-familiar, dreadlocks-must-also-equal-Wacky-Buffoonish-Negroes narrative: Witness the introduction of dreadlocked actor Doug E. Doug in the independent film *Hangin' with the Homeboys* in 1991. Offscreen, Mr. Doug appears to be a thoughtful, college-educated young man born in Brooklyn, New York, raised in the Bedford-Stuyvesant neighborhood, committed and active in the community. He is a gifted mimic, and he comes by his facility with island patios honestly; his family is from Jamaica. But I have to say it: Onscreen, he's a clown. If Screwface, the head Scary Jamaican Negro in *Marked for Death,* recalls the black brute stereotype from films like *Birth of a Nation* and countless others, then Doug E. Doug willingly marries the dreadlock hairstyle with every twitchy, grinning, hysterically fearful minstrel figure you've ever seen. He not only plays "Willie" in *Hangin' with the Homeboys,* he refines his Sambo-dread persona with the role of Sanka Coffie in *Cool Runnings.* Then he takes the persona deeper when he plays "Bernie," the voice of a Rastafarian jellyfish in the animated feature *Shark Tale.* Who would think someone could make a career out of playing clown-dread?

• • •

In another episode from that same season of A Different World, *Jalisa is upset with Coach Walter Oakes. Walter insists he knew it was Jalisa all along when, disguised as "Lisa," Jalisa used a Jamaican accent to flirt with the coach over the phone. She refuses to believe Walter until he goes out the door and then bounds back into the room wearing a long, flowing dreadlock wig and a huge, mischievous grin. He's carrying an African drum and, accompanied by three more dreadlocked drummers, he chants, in his own mocking, broad Jamaican accent, the words "Lisa is Jalisa/Lisa is Jalisa," until she realizes he was telling the truth....*

We're into the early 90s, and dread pop culture references still abound. It's still the golden age; provocation remains the order of the day, but the gold is beginning to tarnish a little bit. *A Different World* featured a joke that would seem extremely obscure, since it demands specific black cultural knowledge. To even have a chance at understanding the joke—since the word "hair" is never used, let alone "dreadlocks"—you'd have to know that Dippity-do is a hair-styling gel popular with black folk, and that Rastafarians don't need it, because they don't comb their hair. It says something that the joke was made to millions of viewers. The writer (who was the then-unknown Orlando Jones, future star of movies like *Drumline*) must have assumed viewer-wide knowledge of black hair in general and dreadlocks in particular. And *that* suggests that dreadlocks were beginning to lose their provocative intensity. Especially since clown-dread, following a straight line down from Nat E. Dred on *Fridays*, was alive and well in the characters of people like Doug E. Doug. A windy swirl of dread is still kicking up dust in 1991, as artists, writers, and filmmakers continue to engage and experiment with using the style on their person and in their work, but the end of the golden age is near.

Dread Lit Syllabus (v)

The market was packed with couples with young babies, each with a fancier stroller than the last. An African man with strange masklike features and a mop of mangled dreadlocks sat banging on a drum before an audience of sullen white toddlers. He wore a kente-cloth smock and cowrie beads and added an aura of hippie mayhem to the upscale faux-bohemian affair.

Hewitt pointed at him and whispered, "Check it out. That man's not really black. That's a dreadlock wig. And you can see the line of makeup on his neck."

Shocked, I squinted at the man. I edged a little closer, but I couldn't see what Hewitt was talking about. By the time I turned back to ask him, he had disappeared into the crowd of shoppers with George.

I forgot about the African man and settled into shopping…

—Danzy Senna, "What's the Matter with Helga and Dave?"
from *You Are Free* (2011)

Dreadlock Wigs Are the New Blackface

I called the seminar "Blackface!" It was born on a Saturday night, a few days before Halloween 2007. Here's *The Collegian*, the University of Richmond's campus newspaper:

> *Around 1 a.m. on Oct. 28, witnesses said a person was seen walking around the 800 block of the University Forest Apartments wearing a painted black face, a dreadlock wig and large, painted pink lips. Those who saw the person said the costume reminded them of blackface, a style of theatrical makeup that was popular in the United States during the 1800s, and one that carries strong tones of racism in today's society. It was not immediately clear whether the person wearing the painted face was a Richmond student.*

Although we discussed the incident in my Black Vernacular class the following Tuesday, our brief discussion wasn't enough, wasn't nearly enough, so I taught my seminar the following year, and now I regularly teach a course on blackface.

It's hard to believe how literal it all was. The idea of an actor or dancer or social joker intentionally rubbing a facsimile of blackness onto his or her face? And then performing in a fashion that the actor—and that actor's audience—is convinced is synonymous with the way real black people behave? And then to have the worth, the success of that performance based on how closely the actor adhered to this presumed "blackness"? Amazing. Head-shakingly amazing. Unbelievable. Part of what we talk about in class are the remnants, the legacy, the still-quite-visible echoes of blackface—and, yes, it's true, part of that Halloween blackface wearer's costume did include "a dreadlock wig."

The thing about blackface is that both whites and blacks "blacked up," although surely for different reasons. And both whites and blacks wear dreadlock wigs. (Do a Google "images" search for "dreadlock wigs." Just brace yourself beforehand.) It's not as baldly offensive as blackface; I'm not so sure dreadlock wigs are offensive at all, really. The cultural space between the wearing of a dreadlock wig and black and white kids saying, "'sup" to each other—or wearing sagging pants—doesn't seem too vast to me. With dreadlock wigs you don't need to blacken your face—the long, thick locks of the wig carry, like the insides of a boiling black kettle, all the symbolic blackness you need. Lock wigs are about performing blackness, about gingerly trying blackness on—literally: tugging it snugly onto your head and either mumbling some words in a Jamaican accent or joking about ganja—or both—or just walking around, feeling "dread." I'm sure it must be exhilarating. I can't deny feeling something similar when I first got twisted myself—and I wasn't wearing a wig.

But these are wigs. There's no growth phase. No twisting process. Just hold it over your head and tighten it down. The alteration must be dizzying. The wig wearer's body is transported to a whole other cultural reality. The lure must be that feeling, that sense of morphing transition, that sense of being altered, being *changed*; it likely resembles what those who blacked up must have felt during the minstrel era. Being delightfully cloaked. Being magically masked. Being gratefully unleashed from the constraints of conventional American society: *Here's my chance to dance my way/out of my constrictions.* One nation under a wig. "Wearing" the culture of an "other." Disappearing into a particular form of blackness—for a moment. Because both blackface and lock wigs carry with them—by virtue of instantaneous removal—the ability to quickly depart, at will, from that form of blackness, as well.

The thing about safaris is that one day they'll be over.

The General Black View of What Dreadlocks Mean Today, More or Less

Standing in front of an Algerian restaurant on Brattle Street in Harvard Square in Cambridge, mingling with Junot Diaz and eight or nine others, all of us having just completed dinner after Diaz's fiction reading down the street at the Loeb. An older, established, very well-respected Latina writer makes a point of singling me out near the curb and shaking my hand, during which she looks deeply into my eyes and says,

"I love your hair."

The unmistakable message I took from her gesture and words was, *Good for you. Step outside of the (white) mainstream. Show 'em. This is ours.* There was a strong sense of the I'm-proud-of-you in her expression, perhaps that more than anything else. It was gratifying, and, at the same time, just a touch unnerving. Yes, it was a small part of what I was doing, and, yes, I was having a good time doing it, but I didn't exactly intend growing my locks to mean a Grand Political Statement, either. Maybe a (lowercase) modest political statement. Regardless, I can't squelch the reaction and pleasure folks like this woman bring to my hair, and I wouldn't want to try. Just a weird moment, that's all. Not bad, not a problem, just unexpected and odd, pleasurable and off-putting at the same time.

• • •

A family friend who lives in Richmond visited us in Worcester with her daughter the year after I got twisted. She arrived, walked into our kitchen, and as I turned around to hug her she saw my hair. She stopped short, threw her fist in the air, and, with obvious pleasure on her face and in her voice, said,

"Right on, brother!" And *then* we hugged.

It was humorous, of course, and we all laughed, but it just flat would not have occurred to her to revive the appropriate 60s reaction to a large, revolutionary Afro and fold it into her 90s spontaneous reaction to dreadlocks if, for her, there wasn't a connection. Obviously there is. I think that's emblematic of the general black view of what dreadlocks mean today, more or less.

The Pure (v)

"It's longer," Jordan said, as she coltishly pranced around Michelle's chair at Roots 'n Locks, watching my post-shampoo retwist in progress. She said it as though my hair had grown an inch during the time I'd spent in the chair. It might have seemed that way. It's really the new growth that has to be dealt with. Some of the hair that has emerged from the scalp since the last appointment doesn't behave itself, it just sits there, just outside the skull, and it needs to be gathered and twisted into the slowly forming lock. Actually, over the two weeks since my last appointment, the new growth had advanced in a particularly hostile manner and then conquered my scalp, triumphantly sticking its colonial flag into my head. Soon it felt as if tiny colonists were sticking their little flags all over. So I scratched. I had to. I'd resisted as long as I could. And when I inspected my fingernails I saw the oily, disgusting dirt that had come off my scalp. I had to get something done, at any rate, and the rate turned out to be 50 more dollars.

As I sat in Michelle's chair, just after my shampoo—I never got tired of getting my hair shampooed—I felt the now-familiar tugging and twisting, tugging and twisting, starting at the bottom of my neck and heading up, row after row. Oddly, out of the corner of my eye, I could see Michelle's hand flash toward the counter next to her, and then she'd continue softly tugging and twisting, tugging and twisting.

After a short while, I realized what might be happening, and I said, "Michelle. You're not putting wax in my hair, are you?"

"Yes, I am," she said, surprised. "You don't want me to put wax in it?"

I tried to mute my annoyance. "Nah," I said, my heart pounding as I forced myself to sound at ease, "no wax. Just use water, okay?"

Where were the alarms? Nobody shouted, "Red alert!" No blinking lights, no whoooop!-whoooop!-whoooop! warnings. No sirens. The radio continued to blare, instead of an urgent tone interrupting the music, with a deep-voiced announcer saying, "This is the Emergency Broadcast System. This is *not* a test." I would have expected, at the very least, a black-uniformed, jack-booted, semiautomatic-rifle-toting Natural Black Hair Security Force to rappel down the building and crash through the windows like John Shaft, showering the shop with shards of glass. "Wax encroachment!" the captain would bark, as the rest of the team leveled their guns at Michelle, her still-waxy hands slowly rising into the air. "Back away from his hair, ma'am. Back away slow."

I'd been compromised. Invaded. Violated. I'd stopped her before she waxed my whole head, but I'd definitely been compromised, no question.

The End of the Golden Age

1992

Talking to her audience during her stand-up show, comedian Bertice Berry says, "I don't look like Whoopi Goldberg. People confuse us because we're both black and have dreadlocks. The other day a lady on the bus said to me, 'You look just like Whoopi Goldberg.' I told her, 'You're fat and white, but you don't look like Mama Cass!'"

The joke is unintelligible without understanding Whoopi as the mainstream standard-bearer for non-Rastafarian dreadlock-wearers—just as the joke also demands a visual familiarity with the expansive Mama Cass of the 60s folk group The Mamas and the Papas. It also acknowledges a world-weary sense of how often whites try to compare blacks to each other. From *Ebony* magazine: "Berry uses the [Mama Cass] gag to make her point, and she still marvels at the response it brings. 'Sometimes I say, "Wait a minute, that line was for me,"' she says with a laugh." Such black audience reactions are about possession: They're about cleaving to blackness in a world that seems to want to reduce and contain physical attributes like dreadlocks when most black folk would prefer to retain the expansive, multilevel cultural resonance of the hairstyle.

• • •

And so the construction is now complete. The golden age has long ago ended. The truth can now be told. One person launched the hairstyle, one person brought it to the American mainstream, and one person destroyed it. The crucial, iconic, vitally important dreadlock-wearers have now been established, and there are three: Bob Marley, Whoopi Goldberg...and me.

Locked

Closer

I wish I could shrink myself to tiny size and stroll my head like I walk the earth. Say someone took tweezers and air-dropped me onto the back of my neck, and I disappeared up into the wilds of my hair. Each individual hair would be like the trees in a forest. I'd love to have a scalp-eyed-view of my hair. From the inside. Not inside the hair itself, but at the very point where it comes out. The follicle, up close, would probably look pretty gross—I wonder if the hair emerges straight out of the edges of the hole, or if there's some play, some sort of naked-to-the-eye-unless-you're-this-tiny goo that surrounds the shaft, allows it to pulse out of the follicle.

I'd get as close as I could to the edge of the follicle, and I'd touch that one hair coming out of the scalp. I imagine that it's hard to the touch, a little slippery, something like sweaty glass. Could I hug it? I'd like to hug it. I'd like to rub the stubble of my beard against a large, tree-trunk-sized black shaft of hair. I couldn't get my arms all the way around, but a good, firm hug, an affectionate hug? I'd like that.

It'd be dark on the surface. I'd be so small that the hair would block out the sun or any light source. It'd be like walking in between those Richard Serra sculptures at the Bilbao Guggenheim. Dark. I'm thinking it'd be like a rain forest, but the only time I'd feel "rain" would be when the water gets squirted on me for twisting. Standing on the surface, I can't imagine I would be able to see the bend of spiraling black hair; it'd be a trunk. So I'd step back from the one strand I was hugging and look up (I couldn't step too far back, though, because I'd hit another hair-trunk). I might be able to see the beginnings of a bend, as the hair ribbons and turns, ready to meet the rest of its community in order to meld. But even then, it's still distinct, it's still its own entry. No matter how much a chorus blends, no matter the melody, it's an assemblage of singular, distinct voices, and my dreadlocks are a permanent melding of millions of strands of my hair, and if I was small enough to hug and admire and stand next to one of those millions, it would still be just a singular one of those millions.

Could I climb my hair? I was a pretty good tree-climber in my youth, but I did need a toehold, a branch, something with which to hoist myself up. I'm not like those coconut-tree climbers who can just throw their thighs and arms around a trunk and shimmy their way up. What if two strands were so close—and firm enough—that I could lean back against one and place my feet against the other and climb that way, like inching up between two close buildings? Might I climb high enough to see the light?

I'm doing it. Using two bulky strands, I'm climbing my hair. Higher and higher, getting closer to the light....

Intimacy

From the sublime...

We were in the kitchen, and I was cutting Garnet's hair. Boy's thicket was right bushy, compared to where it usually was. I was spinning Duke Ellington's second version of *Black, Brown and Beige*, and we were cooling it, just the two of us, myself and my son. There's just something about hair. It is intimate. Even a silent haircut is a form of tactile, one-on-one communication—between cutter and cuttee, braider and braidee, twister and twistee.

. . . to the ridiculous:
Garnet was doing fine, sitting (relatively) still, talking about this and that, when up jumped the devil: "Daddy, can I have dreadlocks—like yours?"

I could've sworn I even heard Mahalia Jackson hiccup for a hot second.

"Well, you know, Garnet, dreadlocks are a grownup hairstyle."

"But I'm *four*."

(That was his rationale/exhortation for everything. Earlier that morning, as one of Jordan's friends had settled into the car as we headed to gymnastics class at the Jewish Community Center, the first words out of his mouth—before she was even in the car—was, "Christine: I'm *four* now.")

"Yes, you are," I said, continuing to apply the clippers. "But I'm talking about even more grownup than four."

"When I get your size, I can have dreadlocks, right, Daddy?"

"Garnet, when you're my size, you can have any hairdo you want."

And the thing is, he's a big boy: He just might be "my size" and still be a good ways away from "grownup," y'know?

Truly, just the idea of supervising Garnet getting dreadlocks was an extremely exhausting thought in that moment. I was having enough of a time with my own.

The Black and White of It

Black hair does twirl its way out of black heads. And so our hair will, indeed, lock together like lovers walking arm in arm down a city street. But just because black hair is circular doesn't mean black hair is the only hair that locks. Visit any skid row district of any major city and you'll see the matted, confused hair of desperate panhandlers and the mentally ill. Or visit the hip part of that same city—often also populated by the homeless and the ill—and you'll see matted or locked hair on young white kids. Cambridge, Massachusetts, is just such a place.

I was on my way to a Zadie Smith fiction reading in Cambridge one day, but I'd decided not to drive. I love Cambridge; I hate trying to park there. I drove to the nearby Fresh Pond parking garage and took the "T," planning to get off at Harvard Square. I waited, the train came, I boarded. I had just sat down, ready to open my *Boston Phoenix*, when two teenaged white girls who boarded after me gasped with pleasure, and darted straight toward me. It took me back to my mini-fame days, actually, when I lived as a more-or-less public figure as a disc jockey in Alexandria, Louisiana. I was happy I had some context for their reaction, or else I might have felt uncomfortable, the way I often had in Louisiana. But they were *so* excited and exclamatory that I couldn't help but smile.

That's all they needed. One had a jacket with patches all over it, the other was generously tattooed, and clearly both were trying, gamely, to grow dreadlocks. "I *love* your hair!" Jacket breathed. "It's *so* cool."

"Thanks."

"How'd you do it?" asked Tattoo.

Now, there are two schools of thought regarding whites and black culture. According to one prominent school, my reaction should be, *What do you mean, "How'd I do it"? I have black hair—it locks because that's what black hair does.* I should say this snappishly, according to this school, irritably, weighed down by centuries of instances where, as (white) actor and playwright Danny Hoch once put it, white people demonstrate that they might love black style, while not necessarily loving black people.

It's the rubber question, one that black people everywhere confront every day: It's the school of thought that says, *Why do* you *want it, white girl? Can't we have anything to ourselves? You want this, too? Damn—leave me alone!* It's the school of thought that Richard Pryor had in mind when he suggested that black men "hold their dicks" because "y'all have taken everything else."

The other school of thought is one that says, *Of course I understand, well-meaning white person—black culture is so attractive, so compelling, so engaging that you want "in," you want to be a part of it; you can't help yourselves. I get it, and I understand. So help yourselves to the buffet of black culture—pick and choose. It's all you can eat, folks. Stuff yourselves.*

But understand this: It's gonna look different when you do it, whatever it is, continues that second school. *You can Afro-frizz your hair in the 1970s, but it's not going to look like Huey P. Newton's Afro. Bo Derek can braid her hair in cornrows til six becomes nine and back again, but it won't look like my daughter's cornrowed hair when Val tightens her up. So go ahead. Eat up. Want some more? Have a fifth helping of blackness. Please. Just make sure you credit the source.*

That's what makes me crazy. Everybody's heard "Alexander's Rag Time Band"; who's never heard of Irving Berlin? But it took the soundtrack of *The Sting* in the 70s to reintroduce America to Scott Joplin. Every kid in America wears ball caps, often backward. But do they know who popularized that style? The banjo is an African instrument—complete with an African name (*bahn*-jo)—but how many people know that? That's what was on the table, for me, when these all-too-well-meaning white girls, without a clue as to what they were really asking, essentially said, *Take our hands and lead us into blackness, please, sir. We've gotta have it.*

And yet, it's astonishing the number of white people who see my dreads and tell me they used to wear the style. These are, often enough, quite conventional white folks who, when I ask, say they cut them to get a job or because they were graduating or some such other rite of passage. When white people get dread, they're walking on the wild side. As are blacks, obviously, in some important but critically different ways. But if I ever cut my locks—should they ever deign to lock up in the first place—I'll still be black. When they cut theirs, they're white. It ain't exactly the same.

There I sat on that "T" train, the embodiment of the black male outsider, arguably the most compelling figure in American culture, the "envy of the world," as Toni Morrison wrote, sardonically, in *Sula*. For those young whites who see dreadlocks as symbolizing the latest incarnation of the black male outlaw figure, the urge to adopt the style must be well-nigh overpowering. It certainly seemed that way for these two young girls, with their window-pane-wide, eagerly anticipatory faces. And so I'm supposed to—what—*help* this poor child, this innocent girl who probably thinks (and why, in this so-called "post-race" era, shouldn't she?) that society sees our heads as exactly the same? Do I help her? Do I give her a hand, help her up to the very Mt. Dread I'm trying to scale myself? Or do I turn coldly away?

• • •

I helped her. I pleasantly answered her questions, knowing full well that as hard as I struggled with my hair, she'd struggle even harder—because her hair doesn't grow in circles like mine does. And even when she has it, even when, if she sticks with it, she's locked up, it won't look like black dread—it simply won't. I suppose what I felt was akin to a veteran pro football player giving advice to a high school kid he knows will never compete for his job. What's the loss?

We chatted easily about process as the train rocked gently from side to side, inevitably rolling us closer to our destinations. They got off, and I started reading my *Boston Phoenix*, shaking my head in amusement, when I should have been shaking my head at myself: How could I know that just by growing my locks I was endangering the style? And if *I* was stalking dread like a hockey-mask-wearing degenerate in a teen horror flick, what did *their* pursuit of the style mean? I wondered idly if I should have discouraged them. Would that have helped preserve the edgy lock-style? Or *is* there no preservation?

I sighed and looked out the window into the underground blackness.

Hair Drama (iii)

As I thought about those two girls, I couldn't help thinking about something Val had told me when she'd returned to Worcester from shuttling the kids back home from their summer in Los Angeles. At the time, Garnet was wearing the buzz cut he'd worn most of his life. It had happened at Disneyland. Val, Garnet, and Jordan had walked into the waiting area for one of the rides, and the ride attendant, some Southern California teenaged white girl, saw Garnet, squealed with delight, and began to *rub his head*, repeating, "Good luck! Good luck! Good luck!"

Val stepped to her. Grabbed her wrist. Got up in her face. "Don't do that," she said, through clenched teeth.

The girl quickly began falling all over herself, apologizing profusely. But Val was still bothered about it, and so was I. She was sorry she didn't report the incident to the girl's supervisor. I wish she had, too, but I know all too well how hard it is to think of exactly what to do when you're in the moment, when a cultural drama is unfolding in real time.

But even though the girl apologized, the question remained: What was all that about? Where'd that come from? Whenever I've argued that black hair is, indeed, a window onto American cultural attitudes and mores, as when Lisa Jones writes, "Everything I know about American history I learned from looking at black people's hair," people usually seemed skeptical. But there it was: A suburban, Orange County white girl loses her mind while working at Disneyland, of all the places for an American cultural drama to unfold. It was as if my family had unwittingly walked into an edited-out scene from Darius James's *Negrophobia*. She was blithely taking tickets from tourists as my wife and kids innocently ambled toward her workstation. When she spotted the hair on my son's head, some historical bubble was released deep in her subconscious. The bubble popped when it hit the surface, and it was ugly. Garnet was an inadvertent, unwilling participant in a real, live American minstrelsy flashback.

It was painful. He didn't deserve that. He was clueless. He was *four*! A cultural cloud of American racial-historical assumptions settled around his unknowing head as he walked through that ride's door. He didn't even have the context to know that he was being violated (the fact that on the grand scale of "violations" this was a relatively minor one was of little comfort as I played the scene out, over and over, in my head. He wasn't scarred by the incident, but I think I was). He was completely innocent, standing there under those rubbing hands. I admire Val's restraint in not slapping the girl, but a small, vengeful part of me sure wishes she had.

Dread Lit Syllabus (vi)

Curses, curses, for those who must touch…

May La Migra handcuff the wait staff

as suspected illegal aliens from Canada;

may a hundred mice dive from the oven

like diminutive leaping dolphins

during your Board of Health inspection;

may the kitchen workers strike, sitting

with folded hands as enchiladas blacken

and twisters of smoke panic the customers;

may a Zapatista squadron commandeer the refrigerator,

liberating a pillar of tortillas at gunpoint;

may you hallucinate dreadlocks

braided in thick vines around your ankles;

and may the Aztec gods pinned like butterflies

to the menu wait for you in the parking lot

at midnight, demanding that you spell their names.

—Martín Espada, "For the Jim Crow Mexican Restaurant in Cambridge, Massachusetts Where My Cousin Esteban Was Forbidden to Wait Tables Because He Wears Dreadlocks"

The Pure (vi)

The fantasy of purity is appalling. It's insane. What is the quest to purify, if not more impurity?

—Philip Roth, *The Human Stain*

It was the night before my first hair appointment of the fall, and I was languid. I sat in the living room in the dark after the kids had gone to bed, thinking about what I would face the next day. My languor was hard to figure, actually, since I could barely keep my hands out of my head. It was pretty much open season on scratching, really. I knew I was getting shampooed and retwisted the next morning, so it was no big deal if I scratched—I knew I'd look fine the next day around noon. Even so, it had been so long since I had a legitimate shampoo that whenever I did scratch I pulled the now-familiar brown, greasy goo away from my head. And you know me: I couldn't help inspecting whatever was beneath my fingernails. Not looking, for me, would be like asking winos not to wine—or asking children not to whine, for that matter.

Maybe my being compromised a month earlier was for the best, after all. I had decided a few days earlier that on my next visit I wasn't going to merely get my usual touch-up. I was going to get shampooed, I was going to get retwisted, and then—I paused for the clap of thunder, the terrified actress, and the high-pitched scream—I was going to tell Michelle to put beeswax in my hair.

I'm going to do it. I stood and jammed my fists deeper into the pockets of my robe as I looked out the living room window into the darkened street. *I'm going to do it. I have to.* It had been a month since my purist meltdown, and I'd had a lot of time to think. *I can do this. It'll be okay.* I didn't just cave, although I guess I did cave. But I didn't "just" cave. I had done some research, and I based much of my decision on something I'd read on the internet. The website, from England (including, of course, British spelling), was simply titled "Dreadlocks." The site contained, at long last, a tight, nonjudgmental, well-documented essay on the process and maintenance of dreadlocks. It was exactly what I'd been looking for. This brother weighed in big on the "locking process." His most important words were these:

> *You won't get locks after waxing your hair once, so you have to use it continually until you can tell something is stuck together and the whole thing is on its way (a guess is that will take—at least—a month). Once you realise you have serious locks coming you should stop adding more waxe. If you continue you might cause an 'overload,' which in its worst case will cause the hair to break and you wouldn't want that. A middle stage here is that you can catch a glimpse of something white-grey-yellow somewhere inside a lock if you look carefully. But even for this to occur you have to put a lot of waxe in there. Waxe smells a bit, but it doesn't really smell bad.*

When I read that, I decided to do it. Fact is, I was still very much bleeding money, like a dread hemophiliac. Michelle and Nicole would be perfectly content to twist me up with water every other week at a hundred a month, and who can blame them? I was the one who needed the financial tourniquet; after their initial surprise, my "natural" fixation didn't bother them in the least. So I decided to get waxed. As my hair grew, it would, I hoped, quickly get to the point where I didn't need the wax, and at that point I'd discontinue. I felt that as long as I closely monitored the frequency of the wax applications, I wouldn't have the unpleasant side effects our humble narrator speaks of above. After all, I desperately needed a shampoo, and was set to get one the next day. I expected the retwist—with "waxe"—would allow me at least a month in between visits. I could only hope.

I looked out into the darkness. So—did this mean that B.J. would be ashamed of me? Part of me couldn't believe I was even asking myself this question. I'm a grown-ass man. I make my own decisions. The problem was, even though I did make the ultimate decision, even though it was my choice, I couldn't help wondering about The Pure—about my commitment to natural dread. Wasn't introducing wax to my hair, after taking such a hardcore stance against it, a little like Alice Walker writing a novel that had "Flyy Girl" in the title? Wasn't it something like McCoy Tyner jumping onto the fusion bandwagon—after having previously played with John Coltrane, no less? Well, yes and no. While B.J. was, indeed, a passionate evangelist for natural locks, was I? I never meant to be. I probably made a mistake going to Twist and Shout in the first place, since she couldn't maintain my locks, first-twist to dreads and beyond. She tried to tell me how important that was; I wish I had known enough to take her more seriously.

If I had originally gone to Roots 'n Locks and they had said that wax was the way to go (and they obviously would have), well, I'd've gotten waxed innocently, willingly, and completely without anxiety. But I had, if nothing else, become aware of the dangers of excess wax, and since I also had a prophylactic—*quit early*—I was actually in the best position to get waxed. And so I decided to go ahead. Guilt free. (Well, guilt lite, anyway…)

A Style Signature

When I'd gone to Washington for that Sterling Brown conference, I was just another twisted-up head of black hair in funky, freaky D.C. The style might have been somewhat unusual in Worcester, but in Cambridge, in Providence (or at least at Brown) and in D.C., I was just another schmoe with dreads-in-training. One thing I'd noticed, though, upon close inspection of folks whose hair had actually completed the locking process, is that on almost every head, the individual dreadlocks weren't locked immediately from the scalp out. The hair close to the head that wasn't locked was the "new growth," and that observation only solidified my insistence that after I'd gotten waxed I wasn't going back to Roots 'n Locks anytime soon. I had decided that I wasn't going back until nearly 1999 or until I was fully locked up, one or the other.

My intensive dread research had informed me that the head produces oil in connection with how often the hair is shampooed. For the previous three months, I had only been shampooing my hair once every three weeks or so, and for the first few months the oil and dirt were as stubborn as heartbreak in a Billie Holiday song. But since I got waxed, not only was I able to go a full month since my last appointment, I felt as if I could have gone even farther. Not only that, but my hair was actually getting pretty long. So I decided to give it the time and space to lock up, minus the retwisting, and see what would happen.

Ever since I'd Twisted and Shouted a little over four months earlier, I'd been reminded that I was growing dreadlocks two ways: by the feel of my hair when I touched it and the reflection of my hair through the eyes of the world. After that most recent touch-up, though, a new phase had been inaugurated: movement. Add one sure reason I was reminded I was growing dreadlocks: I could actually feel them on my head! If I whipped my head too quickly in one direction or another, my hair would arrive a split second later. Or they would hang over my ears in noticeable ways. Or dangle over my forehead in somewhat annoyingly noticeable ways. That's just how long it had gotten. Certainly, it was long enough to lock up if it wanted to.

So I decided I would skip my November appointment, with intentions on waiting through December, too, if needed, in order to let the locks lock. I felt like I could take the pain. My oil buildup was much slower than before, and also I was just flat more used to dealing with an itchy scalp. I thought I might have Michelle twist up my roots a bit if I needed it, but that'd be it: Nobody was going to retwist my starter locks again. It would just be maintenance from then on. I was ready to let nature take its course, however complicated that course might be, due to my including wax in the touch-ups.

Meanwhile, during a rare shopping expedition, I had spotted some T-shirts for sale, black ones. All the rest of the day I thought about what to do. It was like that moment in Jess Mowry's story "Big Bird," where Ryo, referring to airplane flight—and joining the drug trade—says that there's a point of no return at a key point during takeoff. Pilots reach a spot on the runway where they must commit. Either the plane gets nosed into the air or flips, crashes, and burns on the ground. I was in the cockpit, hands at the controls, and, stylistically, I could fly or crash. I took off. And the man who helped me into the air was none other than Reverend O.C. Smith.

I had been talking with my parents at lunch about my sister Pam and her wedding plans. She was going to have it at her church, and O.C. Smith, her minister, was going to officiate. I recalled when Reverend O.C. was a soul music star, and I believe I began humming "Little Green Apples" before I asked my parents, "Does he still wear those little short-waisted suits?" They both chuckled and nodded. Moms: "You *know* he does…" And then Pops riffed, "…and he's still got those high-heeled shoes, too; *and* he's still wearing long hair."

"I like that," I said to them. "I like the idea of having a style signature and keeping to it."

And that was it. That right there. I needed to make my own statement. And since I had a direction I wanted to head in, I needed to keep my head to the sky—I needed to take off.

When I returned to the house the next afternoon, I'd copped a pair of black shoes and five black T-shirts. I wanted to be able to wear black tees whenever I wanted to. If I wasn't wearing a tie, I wanted to be wearing a black tee. Now, obviously black T-shirts aren't as much of a statement as unexpected tie-wear or wearing all-black-all-the-time, but *I'd* know that I'd have a style statement. I didn't know if it would be noticeable. I didn't think I needed it to. I hoped not.

They Can't Stop Me (iii)

The Tuesday afternoon before Thanksgiving, Val and I and the kids drove toward Richmond all evening, arriving at Niecy's at two in the morning. The big problem I had with my hair was that Michelle had inadvertently twisted the locks in the front to fall down over my forehead. Not only was it a pain having Val tease me all the way down the eastern seaboard about having "bangs," but any and all attempts to retrain them so that they'd lay backward on top of my head were completely unsuccessful. I'd even tried a do-rag; I'd been sleeping the last few days with a knotted leg of one of Val's old stockings on my head to try and force the locks backward. It didn't work. Nothing worked.

Well, now, that's not exactly true, either. No, it didn't "retrain" them, but what did happen was that instead of these four or five locks hanging down just above my eyes, they fanned out over my head. It looked like a Basquiat crown. And...I liked it. It looked wild, even though, on the whole, I did have fairly orderly (not to say "pseudo") twists, almost-locks. The chaos, the aesthetic tension between an increasingly "wild" do and otherwise pleasant dread did make for a cool head of hair, if you asked me. Truly, I had been *this* far away from heading back to Roots 'n Locks to have Michelle retwist them so that they headed backward. But every time I caught myself in the mirror, I liked the way they were hanging. Somehow, surprisingly, I liked them wild.

Standing and chatting with the pastor's wife after worship services at First Baptist (Centralia) in Richmond...

"I like your Afrocentric look," she said, brightly.

Minutes later, creeping forward in First Baptist's crowded, after-church lobby, a tall, corporate-ready, clean-cut brother whom I've always liked spots me. His eyebrows fly into the air. He fights his way over and breathlessly looks down at me silently for a few moments.

"Don't you teach at a college that…?" He left the rest unspoken.

"Yes…?"

Staring in horror at the growth on my head, he said, "And they let you…"

I smiled and shrugged. I said, "They can't stop me!"

Slowly, a smile snuck across his face, and he repeated my words, with his own well-how-'bout-that shrug: "They can't stop you!"

We shook hands, laughing, and after a brief conversation went opposite ways.

They Can't Stop Me (iv)

The usual American cultural hangups exist in the academy, too, of course, but structurally and psychologically, there are some stark differences between the corporate world and academe. Fact is, we professors are encouraged to be individuals—up to a point. We're supposed to be as original and nonconformist as possible in our scholarship. (Well, original in content, anyway; we're expected to conform in a huge way to the scholarly formats through which we express our originality.) Same thing in the classroom: Originality of thought is prized, and originality in pedagogy, in teaching method, is prized as well, as long as it works. It's only when we professors come together as committees or make departmental decisions that we're forced to demonstrate a "team" mindset. And even then, it's as a team of individuals—like a golf team or a track-and-field team. Our approach to teamwork is atomistic and individualistic at best. For the rest of the time, let's face it: We offer a pretense of a departmental grouping, under the umbrella of the discipline itself, but we research and publish alone. And the rest of the time, we're quasi-dictators in our individual classrooms.

Dress varies, too, although this is a fairly recent phenomenon. I was trying to find my own sartorial groove, but really, everybody in the academy can pretty much wear what they want these days. I've seen everything from jeans, sneakers, and T-shirts to suits and ties in the classroom. So, yes, we've got far more latitude than the corporate world. But still—style counts, style matters. Always.

Me, I'd been wearing my black tee, some khakis, and my black Timberland kicks. *Am I stylish yet?* I felt stylish, at least a little bit. I think it was the incipient dreadlocks. The whole ensemble would have looked and most certainly felt different if I wasn't growing dreadlocks at the time. But I was, and it tweaked the whole look sideways. I liked that.

• • •

While "they" could not stop me, in all honesty, it didn't appear that they wanted to, either. On-campus reaction had been interesting, most of it coming from the colleagues I'd mingled with minutes before a dinner for incoming students of color near the end of August, just before the beginning of the fall semester. (The students, of course, were innocent; they knew no other me.) One woman walked right up and briskly said, "New do, eh?" Another, standing nearby, thoughtfully suggested that this was a "new image" for me. "Think Andre Braugher will break out in something like this?" she said, folding a quip into a reference to *Homicide: Life on the Streets*, a series we both loved. "So, Bert, tell me," she continued, "*is* this a new do? Or is it a reprise of an old one?"

That was, by far, the most gratifying question I'd yet been asked about my hair. I absolutely *should* have had dreadlocks long ago, during the golden age, even, and I loved the idea that someone would think that I could have had them earlier in my life. Before I could answer, a black male colleague confidentially sidled up to me and said, *sotto voce*, "You know, Bert, guys aren't supposed to say things like this to other guys, but...I like your hair." He went on to ask several functional, procedural questions, questions that seemed to fuse the Envy Factor with the cascade of questions I'd received while I was still in LA during the summer. I was glad I had gotten twisted some time earlier, before I appeared back on campus after my research leave. I'd had a chance to at least begin to get used to not only the hairstyle but the accompanying reactions. By the fall I'd begun to grow into the role; I hope I projected somewhat more been-there/done-that ease as I fielded comments and responses.

• • •

Sitting in the office of a colleague from another department later that same month, chatting about a recent, controversial tenure victory in which the professor was granted tenure when it looked doubtful, my colleague said,

> "Well, the thing is, after a while it's hard to know what you're being evaluated on. I mean, sometimes it seems as if it comes down to the way you wear your hair—"
>
> "Oh, don't say that!" I said in mock-horror, grinning as I interrupted her. She blinked in confusion, and then her eyes flew to my hair and we laughed…

And I could laugh about it, too. Tenure was never a given, it never is, but whatever concerns I had in that respect had, finally, nothing whatsoever to do with hair. A few years later, in 2003, I was enthusiastically and unanimously granted tenure and promotion. Since the semester-opening dinner earlier that fall, a few of my colleagues had expressed delight or curiosity or both. But the overwhelming majority never said anything at all, or never said anything to me, anyway.

I felt no letdown. No disappointment whatsoever. For me, dreadlocks were never really about opposition (not *really*) so much as they were about exploration. And anyway, when a good friend of mine saw my hair for the first time, as I was walking toward Hogan Campus Center, her comment put the perfect, ironic spin on whatever campus reaction I got: "I like it, Bert—it's very professorial."

Homeless

In December, I went to the Christmas pageant at Venerini Academy, Jordan's school. The auditorium was jam-packed with parents of Venerini students, of course, and whoever gazed my way got an eyefull of black-man-with-crazy-dreads. I was more than happy to be sitting beneath them. I just wished they'd lock up already. I was getting impatient. The uncertainty was unsettling.

I had an appointment at Roots 'n Locks for that Friday, and I had her twist the roots of my locks without applying any wax. I wanted to see if I could do without it and just let 'em grow wild.

• • •

I can't police my boundaries, because I can't find them. But God knows I know they're there. I'm like the immigrant who wants to close the borders after him so no one can follow. I'm like the suburbanite who complains of suburban sprawl, irritated that "too many people are moving out here." But I don't have the comfort of ignorance; I know full well hypocrisy stalks me at every turn. I have no right to be a jazz purist. I started across the jazz fusion bridge in 1977, crazy about Weather Report, Bob James, Phoebe Snow, Sergio Mendes, Idris Muhammad. I wandered aimlessly along the bridge, meandering this way and that until I fell under the spell of the Marsalite sect in the early 1980s. Branford and Wynton, Donald Harrison and Terence Blanchard, and early Courtney Pine led me to embrace the entire hard bop canon: Miles, Mingus, Monk, and the rest. I was propelled across to the other side, off the fusion bridge, and I've lived uncomfortably in the land of The Pure ever since.

I don't much like it here. I wish I could live elsewhere. But I didn't choose to live here; my favorites found me and attached to me like Taser-wire. Do we *choose* to like the foods we like? I've never particularly liked pears, and bananas are disgusting—even the sound of someone else eating a banana grosses me out. Food either tastes good to us or it doesn't;

even if we allow for acquired tastes, we have to put in the time to acquire said taste, and even then it's no given. Jazz is what made aesthetic sense to me and continues to sound good to me, to sound fulfilling.

See, I like genres; I can't help it. I like established genres, the same way I like titles and names. Only when generic boundaries are established do I then delight in blurring the hell out of them. What fun is blurring colors to make pink if you can't identify the red and white in the first place? The fact that "pink"—as a color, as an identifier—exists at all nods solemnly to The Pure. I love uncertainty, I love indeterminacy, I love chaos—but I guess I love informed chaos, if that makes any sense (I'm not sure it even makes sense to me). And so I made similarly contradictory demands of my hair: Dread, if you please, but please, dread immediately. The in-betweenness was uncomfortable. It made me feel homeless.

Open Letter to a Dread-Lord

Dear Dreadlocks:

I wonder if this is how children feel, writing to Santa Claus or the Easter Bunny. But then again, when kids write, they're not self-conscious. And I'm always aware, extremely aware, of myself and of these hairy spikes that are taking far too long to solidify. And anyway, children write Santa deeply enmeshed in something that I'm trying desperately to hold on to: faith. Dreadlocks, can you lock me up? Can you finally put me on lock-down, so I can truly open up?

It's like waiting for the final bell to ring on the last day of school. It's like waiting for nightfall on the Fourth of July—or Halloween. How long have I been waiting? It's like walking up to the shorter of two lines and bouncing lightly on the balls of my feet, impatiently watching the longer of the two lines zip merrily along as the person conducting business in my line is underwater—or on Quaaludes. And just before finally getting there, someone goes on a centuries-long search to find a penny—*in order to have* exact change.

It's the night before Christmas every day. It's using a dial-up modem when you're used to cable or DSL. It's turning to stone, as a kid, as you wait for your parents while they stand at the door, with their coats on, "saying goodbye" to host and hostess at a *get-together as night turns to day and back to night again. How long have I been waiting? It's watching wood fossilize. Watching water evaporate. Watching grass grow. Watching…*hair *grow. Slowly. Way too slowly.*

What is it, Dreadlocks? What, am I going to be the first and only person in the history of the hairstyle whom you'll refuse to allow to lock? Why? What did I do? Am I being punished?

That's it, isn't it—I'm being punished. I've been sanctioned. Sentenced. The jury files in as if they're blind and trying to feel their way to the jury box. The bailiff walks through quicksand to the foreman, who is taking forever to stand, slowly unfolding like an origami figure. The bailiff finally gets the piece of paper from the jury foreman and walks as if he, himself, is condemned, to the judge, who reads the note as if she's forgotten how to read, and then hands it back to the bailiff as quickly as if the note weighed 40 pounds. The bailiff heads back to the foreman, walking as if he's a 99-year-old man, and after what seems like 20 years to life he reaches the foreman and hands the note back to him. Speaking in the deep, stretched-out, distorted voice of a slowed-down tape recording, the judge says, "Have you…reached…a ver…dict…?" The foreman nods with the same dispatch the sphinxes have been nodding with for the last thousand years. The judge instructs me to rise, and I do, and the foreman suddenly turns Dread Nazi and screams at me (complete with trilled r*'s): "NO DREADS FOR YOU!"*

The gavel comes down, and there it is: The locking process will never be completed, will it? Just be straight with me, okay? I can take it. Is it because I got waxed? Because I violated the Purist dictum? Is that it? Tell me, Dreadlocks, are you withholding dreadlocks because you didn't like this whole identity experiment idea? Did an old flame from my Louisiana days say something to you? Did she put a root on me? (Lord knows there was enough of that sort of thing going on while I was down there…)

I'll tell you what, Dread—I'm ready. If you could see your way through to actually locking me up—consider this my "appeal"—I'd sure appreciate it. I've been patient; well, as patient as I *can be, anyway. I'm ready to get locked up.*

Dreadlocks? I'm ready.
I'm ready now, Dreadlocks.
No, seriously. For real. I'm ready.
Dreadlocks?

Fuzzy Phase (iii)

A week before Christmas, I washed it. And it—*held together*.

The fear, of course, was that it would all disintegrate—or, worse, integrate—into one huge mass of hair, devoid of wax, devoid of the individuality of twists. But it didn't happen. Maybe it never happens, but I was only concerned with what grew out of my own head. I had made good on my determination to wait until nearly the end of the year before I got shampooed or touched up. I waited, and then, instead of going to Roots 'n Locks, I made like Milkman in *Song of Solomon*: I stood high on the cliff, spread my arms wide, jumped… *and flew*: I shampooed it myself! It looked completely uncontrolled when it was wet, and as if that wasn't enough, as it dried it got hyperfuzzy. Two days later, it was just completely wild, totally frenzied. I had twists that stuck straight up in the air, others that were randomly aimed here and there—something like a disagreeable group of friends pointing to different streets when a stranger asks for directions.

The odd thing is that I would have hated to have had this happen in July or at any other time during the summer, really. And much of the fall. To tell the truth, I'd've been horrified for it to happen at any other time in my entire adult life. I was shocked that I was enjoying it at all. It looked exactly like something I always thought I'd hate but have unexpectedly turned out to love.

Inscrutability (iii)

Standing in the middle of the hallway of Fenwick Hall, short yards from my office on the third floor, having been stopped by a colleague from another department...

> "So, Bert," Colleague said, cocking his head to the side curiously. "When you first came here, you had a short haircut?"
>
> "Yes..."
>
> "And you were clean-shaven?"
>
> "Yes."
>
> "And now you've got shaggy hair..."
>
> "Uh-huh," I said, thinking to myself, *Shaggy?*
>
> "...and a beard."
>
> "Right."
>
> "The thing I was wondering was," he said, pausing ever so slightly, "what does your *wife* think of all this?"

I laughed. I had no idea that was where he was heading. Colleague smiled but didn't join in; it was as if he feared the joke was on him. "Well, it just so happens that my wife loves my hair," I said, when I was able to continue. "As for the beard, in many ways, it's her beard."

He looked at me hard, waiting for me to explain that last remark.

"See, I'd always wanted a beard, but I was convinced I couldn't grow one. And she insisted that I could. So I said, 'Okay, I'll prove to you that I can't. I'll stop shaving for a solid year. You'll see.' As you can see, she was right. And I couldn't be happier to be wrong!"

• • •

Absently pushing my shopping cart around Shaw's grocery store, ignoring the blur of shoppers around me, a red-faced, fiftysomething white woman says something that I don't quite hear, since she's finished by the time I realize she's speaking to me.

> I paused, allowed her to come into focus, returned her smile, and said, "Excuse me?"
>
> And with an apparent mixture of embarrassment and genuine surprise, she repeated, "I like your hair!" As if she couldn't quite believe it to be true.

They Can't Stop Me (v)

The word, just to be clear, is pronounced "boo-jee"—with a soft "j." I've seen spellings ranging from "bougie" to "bouji" to that of my own preference: "bourgie." I've always assumed that the flinging of the term as an epithet began after E. Franklin Frazier severed so many black middle-class heads with his devastating book *Black Bourgeoisie* in 1957.

My own bourgie quotient has always been rather low (at least, as best I can tell), and if so, I come by it honestly: Not only was I not in Jack and Jill as a youngster, I'd never even heard of Jack and Jill as a youngster. The Boule, the Links...I suppose it says something about me and the way I was raised that I didn't know these exclusive, elitist black groups even existed when I was an adolescent. I'd vaguely heard of cotillions and coming-out ceremonies, but I'd heard of bar and bat mitzvahs, too, and I was about as likely to attend both—meaning neither. So it shouldn't be surprising that it wasn't until I began teaching at Holy Cross, at age 36, that I'd even heard of Girlfriends, Inc.

My folks weren't interested in any of that. My father spent his undergraduate years in Los Angeles in the late 1940s, and the way he describes campus life reminded me of Wallace Thurman's depiction of the black bourgeoisie at the University of Southern California in *The Blacker the Berry...*: a stuffy, snooty, brown-bag-test-wielding, bourgie incubator. He wanted no part of it, for him or his family. And thank God for that. His children, as a result, never even had to define themselves against those sorts of attitudes. Now that I know they exist, I have to say I'm not a fan.

• • •

Riding on the New Jersey Turnpike, heading back to Worcester, Val tells me about a friend of hers who was astonished at the black sprouts on my head...

> "Bert is the last person I would imagine doing something like that. He was always so clean-cut," her friend said. Friend thought for a moment and then said, "Well, I guess there always was a little 'Dirty Bert' waiting to come out..."

• • •

And so it must have been Dirty Bert who showed up to deal with the Talking Androids—it was the first term that sprang to mind as Val and I settled into our table to watch a Christmastime ballroom full of burnished, airbrushed, High-Powered Negroes, with puffed-out, helium-filled chests, with only their heavy bankrolls anchoring them to their seats. Talented Tenth? To see these Negroes strut, you would have thought they were the Talented Point-Oh-Oneth. These folk must fart money—or, certainly, try to style as if. No doubt many, many of them could. Beacon Hill elegance. Martha's Vineyard summer houses in the family for generations.

In mid-December, Val and I were invited to Boston's Ritz-Carlton for Paint the Town Red, a fundraiser for Girlfriends, Inc. I couldn't figure out quite where to stand on that Saturday evening. I was the only person in the room growing dreadlocks. I could feel people staring. "Who invited him? What's he doing here? Who is this nigger?"

I loved it. I loved it, even though I have no idea whether my alienation flowed from the outside in or, more likely, from the inside out. When did the transformation happen? Or was it a transformation? I once wondered if I could wear the hairstyle at all. And now, there I was, actually enjoying Basquiat-ready wildness. It's like growing abstract art with my scalp as canvas. Just a few short months earlier I was horrified at the very idea of a "fuzzy phase," let alone actually getting fuzzy. But once I got a taste of being Outsider, I kinda loved it. *Yo, Dirty Bert lives—and he's growing*. My hair, it seemed, was a lens, a magnifying glass. And clearly, just as I suspected, what was inside must have always been there, even if it was hidden. I began to wonder if my urge to try on dreads was, ironically, a way to become *un*masked—just like I thought it might be. Oh, I had big fun that night. Big like the fat, cocky heads of those black elite. This time, there was a spotlight following *me* around all night long. But it wasn't just a circular band of light, it was a force field: I could see out, others could see in, but access was denied. I didn't mingle. I didn't have to. My I'm-not-like-you statement was right there on my head, plain for everyone to see. My hair talked for me that night.

Now, it's entirely possible that I was experiencing one of those all-too-frequent episodes of misreading, moments when I'm microscopically attuned to the reactions of people who couldn't possibly care less about me. Indeed, these Talking Androids, Ishmael Reed's term from his novel *Mumbo Jumbo*, may not have noticed me at all. But I'm pretty sure they did. If I'd had "spider senses" they'd've been tingling. Everyone there was so meticulously attired. So cute. So chic. All the women had gone out and purchased something red; many of the guys wore tuxedoes with red cummerbunds or vests. Nobody grinned widely; this was polite smile territory. Nobody laughed from the gut; a titter or a chuckle was all I heard. And oh my God: not a hair out of place. Ever.

Except on my head. It just so happens that I was in an especially fuzzy and crappy-looking stage of the maintenance cycle. I was near the end of the rotation; ordinarily, I would have long since gone to Roots 'n Locks and gotten my "do did," as Val loved to put it. There were one or two women Painting the Town Red who had tasteful short Afros and who still looked extremely "in." If I had gotten my head waxed before the dance I still would have looked appropriately "out," but it might have seemed as if I had *wanted* to look "right" for the occasion, if not "in." As it turned out, when we got there I was delighted to see that the rough, angry hair I wore made me look even farther "out" than I ordinarily would have. *Hey*, I felt my hair saying to them, *you conform. I go my own way.*

Val and I rode back home, discussing what it was like to chew on this dark upper crust. The last thing either of us would want to do, we agreed, would be to buy into any sort of white supremacist nonsense that suggested that black folk couldn't or shouldn't have money, that none of us was truly upscale, that these Painters of Town Red were all just aping affluent white folk, pretending to be wealthy, simply doing the cakewalk, merely puttin' on airs. That's insane. It was an elegant evening, and it was elegance with a black vibe, unquestionably. No, they were authentically black, all right. It was their attitude that I simply could not stand. Attitude that hovered over that Ritz-Carlton ballroom like a foul scent. The word "pretentious" does come to mind. The very definition of "bourgie."

But wait a minute: What *is* the very definition of "bourgie," after all? Apparently, the word doesn't really exist in any official dictionary, although it certainly lives in the *Urban Dictionary*: "To be pretentious in matters of taste or dismissive of other tastes, in a manner that follows a particular middle class mode of thinking. Generally derogatory." Yup. Sounds about right, except that the definition doesn't deal with what's crucial about "bourgie": perception. See, it's one thing to act bourgie, it's another to be seen as bourgie—sometimes one can be viewed and slammed as being bourgie when that's the furthest thing from one's mind.

I oughta know. I might well have been hit with the bourgie stick now and again, although I obviously see the matter differently. I'm certainly privileged, that's for sure: middle-class, suburban Los Angeles upbringing, higher education, a tenured professor. But does being privileged, in and of itself, make one bourgie? My response to that lies somewhere on the spectrum between *No* and *I don't think so* and *I don't want to think so*.

You know what? Call me Janie: An excellent example of the tension between "privileged" and "bourgie" animates Zora Neale Hurston's *Their Eyes Were Watching God*. Throughout that novel, characters like Nanny, Jody Starks, and Mrs. Turner each had an investment in having Janie feel and express her privilege, to *wear* it, really—the way she "wore" her light skin, her long hair, and, eventually, her inherited money. Whether she was a just-slapped teenager in west Florida sobbing on Nanny's lap; or a full-grown woman in Eatonville where Jody wanted her to shut up, look pretty, and stay off the porch; or even if she was down in the muck, in the Everglades, where Mrs. Turner urged her to "class off"—Janie was privileged, all right, but she simply didn't feel it, and she certainly didn't want to project it. She just wanted to be one of the black *folk*—swapping jokes and stories on the porch, and playing card games and blues tunes in the muck. Is it her fault if she's *seen* as privileged? I mean, really: She spent much of the novel pushing back against other characters' aspirations for her. I see it as another example of that dread-like difference between what you think you are versus how you're seen, perhaps. All you can do is struggle and try your best to be who you are...

So, okay, if all that's true, then maybe I'm being a bit hard on those fatuous Negroes who were Painting the Town Red that night. But maybe not. I can no more peer into the heads of others than anyone can peer into mine. We all walk around, all of us, every day and every night, projecting personas onto others and having others project personas onto us—it's a twisted version of the old Golden Rule. Our clothes, our affect, our demeanor—and our hair—act as a medium between those competing projections, but no more than that. It is what it is.

All told, then, I felt like my hair represented me pretty well that night, as bizarre a notion as that might seem. I was, ultimately, probably indistinguishable from anyone else there in every way but one: My head of rebellious hair flashed a steady neon sign that said, "Well, this brother ain't part of the club, that's for sure." I liked that. I liked that a lot.

Tied Up/Tied Down (iii)

Early the next year I attended the Martin Luther King Jr. Breakfast in Worcester. For some reason, maybe because I came of age in the post-civil rights movement era, events like that breakfast always had me confronting the bizarre duality I've often felt toward my blackness. I mean, I literally had to blink back tears as we all stood up and sang the Negro National Anthem. It was that moving—it often has that effect on me when sung in a group. James Weldon Johnson really nailed the cultural importance, the historical lineage, the sense of our black lives building on past black lives, of our need to make our forefathers proud. Maybe Albert Murray memorably put it best in *South to a Very Old Place* when he called the song the "comb your hair brush your teeth shine your shoes crease your trousers tie your tie clean your nails rub a dub stand and sit and look straight make folks proud anthem!"

"Lift Every Voice and Sing" is like Maya Angelou's "Still I Rise" set to music.

So why is it, then, that at the *very same moment* my Sentimentality Monitor was buzzing, beeping, and clicking like crazy? Let's face it: Dreaded sentimentality, that mawkish mode of expression, almost always surfaces at events like these. I can be deeply moved one minute, and smirking and sighing heavily the next. After yet another ham-handed simplification of the life and message of the Right Reverend Doctor Martin Luther King Jr, my eyes, after they'd rolled in exasperation up to an exploration of the convention center ceiling, rolled back down and settled on Brother Rashaad, from Belmont Street A.M.E. Zion Church, our place of worship when we lived in Worcester. Two Sundays earlier, after church, a serious young man had taken me aside and asked me for advice on how to grow dreadlocks. I immediately looked at his hair and was tickled to see that it was every bit as short as mine had been on that March morning that seemed so long ago. He listened solemnly as I gave him two points of advice: go to Michelle at Roots 'n Locks, and by all means don't use beeswax a day longer than necessary. That helpful "Dreadlocks" website had been taken down, but since I had printed a copy, I told him I would give him one the next week.

The brother looked as unlikely a choice for dreadlocks as I must have been—maybe that's why he wanted them. I had looked for him after church that next week, dread website in hand, and I'd seen him during the service but somehow never saw him after that. So when I ran into him in the convention hall, I told him that I'd have it for him the next Sunday and to look for me. Then we parted. As I walked back to my table, I thought about how and why I'd had to retire my experiment with the tie.

I really did think I could rehabilitate the tie—for my own personal use, at least. It was a crazy idea in the first place. Often a man or woman will marry someone who has questionable behavior in some way or another. "I can change him"/"I can change her," the betrothed passionately insists, often foolishly, in my opinion. I had wanted to do something similar with the tie. In Los Angeles, back in town for my sister's fall wedding, I took it off for the first time since I'd begun constantly wearing them. I walked into Staples Center and took my seat to watch my beloved Lakers play the Toronto Raptors, *sans* tie. In fact, I'd taken it off when I came out of a Borders bookstore in Beverly Hills earlier that day. Why? I'll tell you why: When I was wearing a tie, I was saying to the world, "I'm unique. I wear a tie because I want to, not because I have to. I like the style statement. I'm referencing the past with my tie, as I rock the present with my hairstyle and, wearing both, walk boldly into the future."

Now, that's what *I* was saying to the world as I wore a tie. Here's what I heard from the world, in response: "Do you work here?"

Exhibit A: Val and the kids and I drove out to Springfield, in western Massachusetts, to see the daughter of a friend of the family perform in Up With People. There was a white actor, one of the kids in the show, up onstage playing a college professor. He wore his long hair in a ponytail, and he wore a blue Oxford button-down shirt, off-white khakis—and a tie. And it was the tie, and the tie alone, that separated him from the rest of the kids onstage. If he hadn't been wearing that tie, he would have had little trouble blending in completely. But he did stand out. Because he was wearing a tie. And the sole reason the character, the professor, was wearing a tie? He was at work.

Exhibit B: When I was picking out ties at an LA men's store with my college friend Keith, I asked him about wearing ties. "I pretty much have to," he said, while making it abundantly clear that when he wasn't at work, it would have never even occurred to him to wear one, not for a heartbeat.

Exhibit C: When I was in Boston, browsing for a new suit for the wedding, three different shoppers—two at Filene's Basement, one at Syms—asked me, "Do you work here?"

Exhibit D: Recall my own fascination—and the conclusions I drew—when I saw that dreadlocked brother-in-a-tie walking down Main Street at nine a.m. in downtown Worcester.

Exhibit E: When a woman stopped me in the Borders across from the Beverly Center with the same question—"Do you work here?"—I finally realized that if you happen to walk into a retail store on a Saturday or a Sunday wearing a tie, whether you're in Boston or Los Angeles or Walla Walla, Washington, for that matter, folks are naturally going to assume you work there because, really, just who else in this day and age would be wearing a tie if they didn't have to? Either they're on their way to, or have just come from, or are presently at, *work*.

The idea is ahistorical, really. The wearing of a tie for casual wear is simply out of step with the twenty-first century. It is, literally, *out* of style. I'd've had about as much luck trying to rehabilitate the Members Only jacket. Or the leisure suit. Or the Nehru. Style moves on, and while we are, indeed, in dialogue with previous styles, certain styles can be revised and others simply can't, at least not by oneself. I had seen a PBS documentary on New York City a couple of weeks before we flew to Los Angeles, and it repeatedly showed images from the first half of the twentieth century. All the men were wearing hats. *All of them.* It was both fashion and convention for that era. It's a fashion statement that can be revised and explored today, as well. Wearing a fedora at a jaunty angle can communicate "cool" as much as any other contemporary style statement. By no means am I suggesting that once a particular style has passed on it can never be revisited simply because it's become passé. I have a black fedora, and I did wear it now and then before I got twisted. I was wearing a fedora the night I proposed to my wife. A buddy of mine likes fedoras, as well. But neither he nor I can bring back the first half of the twentieth century. Our hat-wearing doesn't mean the same thing today as hat-wearing meant then. And my wearing a tie doesn't mean the same thing, either.

So I took it off. Sure, I could have stuck with the tie, I could have been table-poundingly obstinate and insisted that I could force fashion, but I didn't want to be stubborn. I wanted to be stylish. You have to know what style is, and then attempt to put your own personal stamp on it—from the inside. Either that, or get so far outside that you completely create your own style (in that case, I believe, it becomes a matter of how well one carries off that outré style, so that how one wears it, in the latter case, is actually more important than what's being worn). But I can't go that far outré—it's just not me.

• • •

And yet, I had also realized all too clearly by that frigid King Day January morning that perhaps radically altering my clothing aesthetic was, similarly, just not for me. I had tried to wear a tie, and the world said no. I had purchased a drawer full of black T-shirts, and a tragic bleaching incident (referred to, around our house, as the Black Tee Holocaust) wiped out almost all of them. But even though there seemed to be a lid on just what I could wear, what I was comfortable with, there was, I'd found, a monstrous advantage to wearing dreadlocks: I didn't have to get dressed when I didn't feel like it. Dreadlocks were a free pass out of ordinary clothing convention. For me, it was mostly "dressy casual" occasions that got exploded. Not the dress-up events, because I never minded getting dressed, and it wasn't a concern for nobody-cares occasions, either, because on those occasions, well, nobody cared. No, it was those public moments when some effort is expected, something like a Casual Friday extrapolated into everyday life. At events of that sort, you're not supposed to just show up in faded Levi's and a ratty T-shirt, even though you're not expected to wear a shirt and tie, either. If I was invited to such an event but I was in one of those rare spaces where I just didn't feel like paying close attention to what I should wear—particularly if I didn't really want to go in the first place—sporting dreadlocks was a real advantage. Dreadlocks are, after all, something of a sartorial force field: Not only do the locks literally shoot out from your head but they figuratively droop all the way down to the soles of your feet, "covering" and providing context for your clothing choices, as well. If I wanted to dress down for an occasion that presumed dressing up, or at the very least dressing "decent," I could throw down my locks-card and disruptively dress *way* down, if I felt like it. I figured the social arbiters would expect unconventionality from me; after all, I imagined them saying, just look at his head!

Ultimately, though, I was surprised at how little I was able to massage my wardrobe. I might have wanted to appear as the New Bert, stunning all and sundry. But the fact is, I still felt uneasy. I knew I couldn't wear louder colors; clothes that were too vibrant simply made turn-of-the-century Bert uncomfortable. They always had, and they continued to do so. Even as I was coming to terms with being stared at because of my hair, I continued to struggle with the accompanying clothing alteration. Once I got twisted, the hair was there, and I had no day-by-day choice. Clothing options, however, were another matter entirely. I had to choose, daily, and even though I wanted to evolve sartorially, I just couldn't bring myself to do so. That's the thing about conformity—it's not just forced from without, it also emerges from within.

• • •

But I did still have my hair. I liked it wild, no question, even though it still hadn't locked up. And then I just upped and shampooed. Bam, just like that. I still constantly looked into the mirror, still peered into an uncertain future style. *But you see that doesn't matter with me now. 'Cause you see I've beennnnnn to the hairline—and I've looked over! I've seeeen the promised head. And so I'm happy tonight. I'm not worrrrried about anything. I'm not fearing…any dread! Mine eyes have seeeeeen the glorrrrry of the coming of the form!*

At Long Last Dread

Mirror in the bathroom, please talk free
The door is locked just you and me…

I don't know what I was expecting. A 250-piece marching band to show up outside my house, blaring a fanfare? To look outside my bathroom window to see a platform and a podium, with dignitaries onstage, waiting to award me, still in my bathrobe, the Welcome-to-Dreadlock Award? A phone call from the president?

I had no firm vision of an endgame. It was a little like being lost in a strange city, wandering around, trying to find a building, and then discovering, as you ask directions, that you were standing right in front of it. I thought I would know. For all this anticipation, I figured I would instantly know when The Day I Was Locked arrived. One day, seemingly the same as any other day, I looked into the bathroom mirror.

I've ripped words from the English Beat's "Mirror in the Bathroom" because, for me, getting locked really was something like that: a mild form of mental illness. Intense, irrational longing. Hoping against hopelessness. And then one day, I gazed into the looking glass and realized…*I've got dreadlocks.* Truly. For the first time I felt as if what I had growing out of my head was actually dread—instead of merely ambitious adolescent twists that would grow up to become dread someday.

I'm locked. I'm locked. I'm locked. I'm locked. A dread mantra; words I'd been waiting so long to hear myself say. And once I started saying it, once it was finally true, I couldn't stop saying it.

I was happy. Really happy. Warmth spread through me like hot cocoa after a winter walk. I loved it. I loved them. Sometimes I'd stand directly in front of the mirror in the bathroom and shake my head, laughing at the way my locks flipped around. It was hilarious. I was delirious. I wanted to say I should have done it sooner, but I couldn't really say that. I did it when I could do it. But I did love the fact that I *had* done it. Just the move itself, as well as the end result, was immensely satisfying. Long may they wave....

Confession (II)

Dreadlocks Is Dead

I intentionally use the seemingly incorrect "is" rather than the grammatically correct "are" to draw a fine distinction between actual hairy dreadlocks atop heads everywhere—*dreads as such*—and "dreadlocks," the vaunted *dread text*, the twenty-first century phenomenon that carries continued cultural meaning, however vast and ill-defined that meaning might be.

Traditionally, the impassioned, aggrieved statement goes this way: "'X' is dead." And so I must not break with tradition. The sentence must read this way: "Dreadlocks is dead."

I'm glad it sounds incorrect; I'm glad "dreadlocks is dead" sounds so jarringly, aurally wrong. That screechy note, that wince-inducing "is" should call attention to the stark difference between "hairy dreadlocks"—which are, after all, just so many slim strands of matter easing out of follicles—and dreadlocks' cultural relevance in the contemporary American reality.

Hip-hop is dead.

The novel is dead.

The internet is dead.

Dreadlocks is dead.

I've always been amused by "...is dead" declarations. Whoever steps out to assert them—and whoever jumps up to deny them—cares, and cares deeply about the subject. "...Is dead" declarations are like a desperate call for help, the stressful signal of a crisis, a crucial, critical assessment that ultimately says, *Something is wrong here, and it may be too late to change it.* Because the hilarious thing about "...is dead" declarations is that they often seem to first come during what appears to be the subject's greatest popularity. (Who among us hasn't heard some version of, "Don't wanna go to that club; it's dead—too many people go there now..."?) I almost always have a "*huh?*" moment whenever I read that "it"—whatever "it" is—is dead. Unless, that is, I care, and care deeply, about the subject.

I care about dreadlocks. I care deeply about dreadlocks.

And dreadlocks is dead.

• • •

I'd've called 911 if you'd had a body to revive. I'd've tried CPR if you'd had a pulse in the first place. How do you rhythmically press the chest of an essence? I saw the lights go out, but did you truly leave? Sure, the style *is still around; it's everywhere. But that core difference, that dread groove—is it there? Did you leave that legacy? The toddler's concentration is palpable as she takes in hand one...more...block...to add to her tower; at the exact same time, with trembling fingers, several states over, a kid gingerly adds one last, fifty-second card onto the scaffolding of playing cards; and that timeless Hungarian family on* The Ed Sullivan Show *somehow flings spinning white plates up onto long, thin poles, vigorously rubbing the poles between palms to keep those plates twirling. Four, five,* six *whirling plates-on-poles, until one...too...many...*

And they all come tumbling down. The blocks in Des Moines. The playing cards in Scranton. The plates in Manhattan. Dreadlocks in America.

Dreadlocks? Dreadlocks, can you hear me? Oh yeah. Of course not. As a vivid, pulsating, cutting-edge hairstyle, you're completely lifeless. Dead.

• • •

So I must confront the question, *What hath death wrought?*

In the years since I killed dreadlocks, there have been two dread-related developments, each, I believe, building on the other: Smugness. And satire. (*Pure? Meet Smug. Oh—you guys know each other? What's that? Can't remember a time when you weren't associated? Uh-huh.*)

I snuffed dreadlocks and then proudly wore the style into the new millennium. But as dreadlocks moved into its post-dread era, heads with dreads seemed to almost exude a smugness that either I hadn't noticed, or that simply wasn't there before. Late in the year 2000 my sister gave me a gift, a book called *Dreads*. And a more precious, pretentious, self-congratulatory, I-got-dreadlocks-and-ain't-I-grand book on black hair I simply cannot imagine. Take, for instance, the Jamaican disc jockey who says, "My body is my temple, I must maintain it in order to exist within this time. Dreadlocks attest to my self-confidence and sanity." Or this, from a Jamaican artist: "In Native American cultures, long hair represents maturity. My locks are a sign of my wisdom." And this, from a "scientist/artist" in New York City: "I'm what you would call a twenty-first-century Renaissance man. I don't categorize too easily.... My dreads acknowledge what I would be were it not for all the things my brain has been taught to do. They're primal, a token of origin." A market researcher in New York City claims, "People see me differently now, they listen more intently. I am taken more seriously and command more attention. Due in part to my dreadlocks, I am seen as a person of substance and integrity."

This sort of I'm-the-dread-king-of-the-whole-wide-world commentary simply did not exist during the golden era. Dreadlocks were still too new. Even the ponderous, explicit links of dread to African heritage that absolutely existed fifteen years earlier were, at the very least, connected to a source—the Motherland—other than sheer vanity and self-regard. In the space of time since, though, along with the marked growth of dreadheads who aren't Rastafari or reggae musicians or Jamaican (or even black) grows the need, it seems, for dread to justify their dread. I understand it, but it still leaves me a bit nauseated. I should have seen it coming, but I didn't. And maybe I'm being dismissive, now, of exactly the sort of dread philosophy that first allowed me to try and get outside of myself. *Difference* is at the core of dread, after all. The Rastas wanted that difference when they adopted locks and gave it the name and dominant meaning in the first place. So as I flipped through the pages of *Dreads*, I wondered briefly if I was being too hard on the people who appear there. Maybe, I thought, they're merely verbalizing what so many people already think dreads mean. And then I read this, from a New York singer: "Dreadlocks express my faith in myself and my culture. They are the pathway to a natural and spiritual life." Did you hear? Not *a* pathway, "the" pathway. And, pages later, when I read this, from an artist who lives in Jamaica, "My dreadlocks proclaim the fullness of creation," I'd had it; I was completely through.

I'm not the only one who's developed a healthy annoyance for dread smugness, either. It was around that same time, plus or minus the year 2000, that something of a dread backlash surfaced. I don't think it's a coincidence that at the same time dreadlocks entered the Years of the Smug, the hairstyle also became ripe for satire. Observe:

> *The big man placed his chin in his hand. "Man, I hate niggers with dreads. A coconut motherfucker, all right, but an American nigger? They too stuck up."*
>
> *"Think they playboys."*
>
> *"But if they didn't have dreads they'd look like plain old mailman niggers from around the way."*
>
> *"Wouldn't be so special."*
>
> *"So fucking spiritual."*
>
> *"So fucking revolutionary."*
>
> *"So together."*
>
> *"Self-actualized."*
>
> *"Bracelet-, bangle-wearing, bitch-ass niggers."*
>
> *"Don't even listen to reggae music."*
>
> *"Most of all you can't trust 'em."*
>
> *"True."*

This short exchange between two characters in Paul Beatty's year 2000 novel *Tuff* has nothing whatsoever to do with the plot. Their critique was prompted by the arrival, on the street, of Spencer Throckmorton, an eight-track-playing, classic Ford Mustang–driving, Loggins and Messina–loving black man who not only grew up in a black upper-class enclave of Detroit but became a Jewish rabbi as well. Upon discovering that Throckmorton wore dreadlocks, Tuffy and Fariq ruminated, in the excerpt above, on the present state of African-American dread.

Dreads have, alas, become a cliché. It's hard to believe how many conversations I've had with dreads and dread aspirants who talk about how eager they are to change their lives—become a vegetarian, give up smoking, become more spiritual—and that growing dreadlocks stands as an elemental aspect of that evolution. Sound familiar?

I'm to blame. It's all on me. If only I hadn't attempted to use dreadlocks to explore the hyphenated space between un- and conventional, I have to believe dreadlocks would still be the cutting-edge hairstyle it once was. You see, *I'm just not hearing* that Beatty's slash-and-burn cultural commentary would have appeared during the golden years—dread's cultural space simply wasn't fully enough defined. But its space certainly is fleshed out now, however contradictory and illusory that "space" might be. Beatty's pungent, pimp-slap cultural critique cements the sad fact that dreadlocks just don't mean what they used to mean. And while it was never particularly clear what they were supposed to mean, whatever they were supposed to mean, they surely mean something different now. Not something bad, not something wrong, but, certainly, something different. Beatty sees dreadlocks as an absolutely credible way for Tuffy and Fariq to "type" Spencer Throckmorton. And so, metaphorically, Beatty takes each of Throckmorton's locks and lights them afire—with a blowtorch. I mean, sure, class distinctions between African Americans always mattered among blacks, but the fact that Beatty can use dreadlocks to hilariously send up a certain type of black person speaks loudly and clearly to the twisted shape of dreadlocks in the African-American cultural imagination deep into the twenty-first century.

"love it lanky; love it loose"

"So, Val—do you like my hair now?"

I used to ask her that every other month or so, just for grins, because although I always hoped for a certain answer, I pretty much knew what I'd get. Her reply, when it came, was always swift and decisive, an echo of my young cousin's response to my humor years before: "No." It was a little ritual I'd concocted over the last few years, a running gag that apparently only I think is funny.

About seven years after first getting twisted, I was still struggling to reach a certain level of psychic comfort. Nearly a decade earlier I had begun a quest, a psychological trek, to see if I could match the outside Bert to what I felt certain was the inside Bert. And all I succeeded in doing, alas, is discovering that I'll never have a perfect match.

I entered a Dread Zone in the spring of 1998. It was something like entering Sir Nose d'Voidoffunk's "Zone of Zero Funkativity"—better known as "The Nose'd Zone." I got twisted, all right. Into knots. And I don't mean the ones on my head. I wanted to go outside, I wanted psychic and stylistic expansion, and yet I knew if I expanded too much, like when you come to the surface from deep water too quickly, I'd get the bends. I got twisted. And the world, which up to that time was spinning on a recognizable axis, was suddenly thrown violently off-kilter, as if earthquakes were the norm, rather than the exception.

I hated it. And I loved it. And I loved hating it, and I hated loving it. I was wholly attracted to the dread I felt. At the very same time I was dreadfully distracted. Call it...productive disruption. Having gone through the house of mirrors that is the "locking process" and emerging, wobbly and trembly, on the other side, I had one more lesson to learn. And in order to learn it, I had to stop twisting my hair.

• • •

Oh, it's still dreaded, all right. I'm not crazy—I didn't say I cut it. I said I'd stopped twisting it. Starting in the summer of 2005, I just let my hair grow for a little more than four years. I thought I'd liberated it. Free at last. Free at last.

I was at a summer seminar at the National Humanities Center in Research Triangle Park, North Carolina, at the time, and my hair had three delightfully confused layers of dread-size. At the very edges were the smallish, thinnish strands that were either what B.J. originally twisted into starter locks or the results of my grim attempts to thicken them—I couldn't really tell which. In the middle of my longish locks was a three-or-four-for-one gathering of dread that was about as thick as a Tootsie Roll. And growing directly out of my head—with absolutely no twisted, attended-to "new growth"—were the bicycle-handle-bar-sized locks that were, at last, the thickness (I thought) I'd always wanted.

I didn't twist them. At all. For four years. I washed my hair twice a month, usually the first and fifteenth, and when I stepped out of the shower and into the mirror I'd dry them off with a towel and go about my business as my locks air-dried. *My hair finds its own way*, I thought; *I'm not guiding it anymore.* And no, I feared no "fuzzy"; I was far less compulsive about control, one of the welcome outgrowths, if you will, of getting twisted in the first place. I cared less how others thought my hair looked, because I'd come to embrace it wild and unruly, as unlikely as that might have seemed when I began the whole process. In some ways I preferred that manner of dread because it separated my head from those exceedingly fashion-dread folks who wouldn't consider for a heartbeat leaving their hair untwisted after they wash it. For them, it was as if they'd been trapped in an ongoing, largely futile quest for elegance and neatness, as if their needles are scratched on fear-of-fuzzy-phase LPs, and the tonearms will never get lifted off the vinyl. *Me, I've learned*, I thought, *through trial and great error, this lesson: Let it go; love it lanky; love it loose.*

• • •

Yeah, well, that was then. This is now. What I hadn't factored in was my flat head. Since I didn't twist the new growth, it grew out flat on my head. I wanted thick locks, but I also wanted them to be tubular, and that just didn't happen. I suppose that was natural, but it didn't work for me. There's a difference between hot dogs and hamburgers, and I wanted hair that resembled the shape of the former rather than inch-and-a-half strips of the latter.

So for the last few years I'm back to twisting up the new growth. I've achieved the tubes of hair I prefer. At this moment I have sixteen locks of varying thicknesses, and about half of my hair consists of the curled-over flatness from before, while the other half, the closer-to-my-head half, is the circular thickness I always wanted. The journey continues.

I'm happy I tried unguided wildness, though. If I hadn't, I wouldn't have finally understood, once and for all time, that "*love it lanky; love it loose*" looks really good as the subtitle of a chapter, but doesn't really work on a head—this head, anyway. I needed to understand that dreadlocks truly are, always and forever, a constructed hairstyle. It just is. Always has been, always will be. It might signify "natural," but it isn't, not really. *My hair finds its own way; I'm not guiding it anymore* is unsustainable and unrealistic—and even those who lock and, once locked, truly do nothing to their hair are still firmly residing inside a style. Always will be.

• • •

I've had less success with my clothing aesthetic, but I've made strides there, as well. As with my hair, I've ended up using subtraction to find that the less-is-more maxim works for me. I almost never wear sneakers anymore. I own no blue jeans. For several years I not only wore no more ties but also rarely wore shirts with collars. I love shopping at thrift stores, where I can buy vintage suits and sport coats and overcoats, most of them having jussst enough of a noticeable imperfection—a slight burn mark here, a missing button there, an offbeat color, a frayed cuff—that marks them as somewhat out of step with the norm. For years, in the fall and winter, I wore black jeans, clunky shoes, and a sport coat; in the spring and summer I'd wear rumpled khakis, sandals, and a light sport coat.

I've been experimenting with color lately. Envision me in black jeans, black socks, black shoes, a black belt, a black sport coat—and a blazing, fire-engine-red T-shirt at the center of it all. Other times I'll wear, say, all of the black above, with a black T-shirt, but underneath that black tee I'll wear an orange or gold tee, so that instead of that triangle of red in the first example, in this second case a slice of color will peek out from underneath the collar, just under my Adam's apple. I've been wearing more colorful shirts lately. I like French cuffs and cuff links—and I wear bow ties, too, still trying to provoke today's version of Ralph Ellison's American joker, just in case Ellison's contemporary representative stumbles upon me while taking an after-lunch stroll. I'm having fun with it.

Dreadlocks for Life

At the end of the day, I'm sitting around with all the other girls, we're all smoking Salem cigarettes, we've got our feet up, we're drinking Coca-Colas, we're talking about the day, and this one other beautician that I loved turned to me and she said, "You know, honey, when you get right down to it, hair is the most important organ of the human body. You know, it's immortal. It'll grow after death. Think about it: hair is one of the great mysteries..."

—novelist Lee Smith, *The Monti* podcast, January 31, 2012

It's funny how, just in that slice of time between now and when I got twisted, people still ask me why I dreaded my hair. But people also now ask me when—or if—I'll cut my dreadlocks off. I have half a mind to tell them that since I'm the single individual whose adoption of the style removed it from the "cool" school for all time, my punishment is that I'm sentenced to dreadlocks for life, with no possibility for hair-parole. I could tell them that these aren't really dreadlocks dangling from my head, they're prison bars—that my head's locked inside them. But I don't say that. I simply tell them that I'll never say never, but I have no plans to cut any time soon.

And anyway, even though I do feel massive guilt about committing involuntary dreadslaughter, I do know that dreadlocks, as the wise beautician above insists, will *grow after death*. The style—if not the spirit—still maintains a doggedly disruptive space in the American cultural imagination. Even though everybody and their grandma wears dreadlocks these days, somehow the style still retains—and, I believe, will always retain—a slight trace of difference.

> *In May of last year, I'm standing at a grocery store checkout station in Harbor City, a suburb of Los Angeles, waiting for one checker to be relieved by another. "Romar," a tall, handsome, charismatic young man who appears to reside somewhere on the Afro-Latino spectrum, is about to depart, but not before he abruptly stops, fixes his eyes on me, and, quite out of nowhere, points at my chest and says,*
>
> "You look like a professor!"

Wha—? Obviously not the first time I've been viewed as "professorial," and surely not the last, either, but it's the first time I've heard it completely out of context, unprompted in any way, thousands of miles from my home institution, and by a total stranger! Inhabiting "professorial" on campus is one thing, being seen as professorial by friends and family is another, but in this case I hadn't even opened my mouth. Even if I had been dressed for the classroom he couldn't have known: I was wearing khakis, sandals, and a burnt orange tee; it was summertime. Maybe it was my demeanor. Perhaps my wearing glasses pressed his "professor" button. And yes, even he was surprised he'd nailed it so well after I blinked, stammered a bit, smiled a shocked smile, and then confirmed that I was, indeed, a college professor. Something had spoken for me, since I hadn't spoken myself. It had to be the locks. It had to be. I don't know what else it could have been.

• • •

The initial television spots for the Valvoline Engine Guarantee program aired on the opening telecasts of the NBA playoffs. In one of the commercials, a white skydiver, decked out in jump-gear, stands uneasily near the open door of his plane, the next to jump. The sky roars outside, and he pauses and turns, and urgently yells over the sound to another man sitting inside the plane, possibly his friend, possibly a jump-instructor or attendant: "Are you sure *the parachute was* packed right*!?" The next thing viewers see is the youngish blond white man the skydiver was speaking to, who is looking confused, as if trying to remember something. Then he brightens, looks at the skydiver, loosens a dopey, toothy grin, raises both thumbs, and slurs,*

"Probably!"

The spot's tagline is, "Sometimes 'probably' doesn't cut it. That's why Valvoline guarantees your engine up to 300,000 miles." I wonder how much it matters that the respondent's blond hair is dreadlocked. He seems vacant and goofy, his helmet is slightly too big, his goggles are askew, and tendrils of unmistakably dreadlocked hair drape his face. The dreadlocks seem to place him in a squishy, nontraditional, crunchy-granola space in American culture, apparently untrustworthy to mainstream society—which then makes him available to be used in contrast to worthy Valvoline, which you *can* trust.

• • •

Around the same time, on an ordinary weekday afternoon, a fortysomething black woman wearing Afrocentric garb—complete with head-wrap—is coming in the door behind me as I enter the Barnes and Noble in Chesterfield Town Center, in suburban Richmond. I was listening to a podcast at the time, wearing earbuds, and so I didn't quite hear her when she first spoke. I hit "pause" as we stood for a moment, just inside the doors. She was asking me if I knew the story of Samson, from the Bible. I nodded. "He had locks, too, you know this?" I assured her that I did know that. Then she carefully looked over my dreadlocks, really taking them in, smiled, leaned toward me, and said,

"Wear them with pride."

It was like one of those moments when you hear a black person say to another black person, "Stay black." Or when someone insists, "Keep it real." The way she said it, it sounded like a request, and a genial request at that, but I couldn't help but hear a hint of a pea-sized threat under layers of cultural mattresses. There's an unspoken concern floating underneath such comments, or else they wouldn't be uttered at all. Somewhere inside that woman existed the possibility that I *wouldn't* wear them with pride, that I might be fashion-dread, that I might not care—that I might not know—about what they meant, about whatever she was sure they meant, anyway. I heard her, on multiple levels, then I smiled, we parted, and I continued into the store.

Dreadlocks are everywhere, these days, on everyone, and yet, apparently, somehow, deep into the twenty-first century, they still carry contested, ambiguous, unsettling meaning that prompts total strangers to offer observations and, in some cases, gentle admonishments. Dread text continues to assert, and continues to be read, long after the golden age of dreadlocks, like a hairline, has receded.

• • •

Here's what apparently hasn't changed: Dreadlocks remain a *Where's Waldo* optical illusion, something that viewers peer into as much as gaze upon. *We're going in*, people still seem to say as they behold dreadlocks, even now, and they bring all sorts of cultural baggage with them to the flight check-in counter. When people I've never met before see me, I'm clearly The Kind of Guy Who Wears Dreadlocks. When people I'd known for years see this different me, they struggle even more than when I grew my hair out, trying to match the me they've always known with their preexisting notions of, well, The Kind of Guy Who Wears Dreadlocks. And so the Me-I-used-to-be morphs and shape-shifts and fades in and out like so much visual static, as if I'm out of phase, scrambled between science-fiction realities.

It was, and remains, a peculiar Ellisonian "invisibility," a twenty-first century site for DuBoisian double consciousness. There's the Bert I feel I am, which apparently differs from the Bert others see, and yet "others" don't, in any way, agree amongst themselves as they contemplate the Bert they think they see when they gaze upon me. Deeper, *I'm* not really projecting the Bert I've matured into, since this dread-style seems to scream things about me that don't quite match the identity I carry inside, but I vibe on that difference, after all. I thrive on that difference.

It's really hard to tell just where the line rests between the Bert I think I am and the quite separate and distinct identity that I've grown accustomed to projecting. I don't think I'll ever be The Kind of Guy Who Wears Dreadlocks, whatever that means, but I am, indeed, a guy who wears dreadlocks—I'm floating in between those two poles, and I'm not at all sure I'll ever be able to strap myself firmly to either one. And anyway, I'm not so sure I want to.

So. It appears that a slightly-less-queasy comfort zone—indeed, a *dis*comfort zone, a sense of dread quasi-equilibrium, is both where I live and what I'm after: a way of allowing the invisible to become visible (to me, if not to anyone else), to the extent that that's even possible…

• • •

Meanwhile, an almost microscopic bit of hair pushes out of my scalp like an idea, like a possibility, even as I write this, even as you read this. Slower than the naked eye can see, it circles up and out and into the air, ready to meet the world, ready to mirror perceptions carried by us all.

Bibliography

Afro-Punk, directed by James Spooner (Chatsworth, CA: Image Entertainment, 2006), DVD.

Barth, John. *The End of the Road*. New York: Doubleday, 1958.

Beatty, Paul. *Tuff*. New York: Alfred A. Knopf, 2000.

Buckley, Peter, ed. *The Rough Guide to Rock*. London: Rough Guides, 2003.

Buxton, David. *The Abyssinians*. London: Thames and Hudson, 1970.

Byrd, Ayana D. and Lori L. Tharps. *Hair Story: Untangling the Roots of Black Hair in America*. New York: St. Martin's Press, 2001.

Carter, Stephen L. "The Black Table, the Empty Seat, and the Tie." *Lure and Loathing: Essays on Race, Identity and the Ambivalence of Assimilation*, Gerald Early, ed. New York: Penguin, 1993.

Chevannes, Barry. *Rastafari: Roots and Ideology*. Syracuse: Syracuse University Press, 1994.

_____, ed. *Rastafari and Other African-Caribbean Worldviews*. New Brunswick: Rutgers University Press, 1997.

Darwin, Charles. *On Evolution*. London: John Murray, Albemarle Street, 1859.

Davis, Stephen. *Bob Marley*. West Sussex: Littlehampton Book Services, Ltd, 1983.

DuBois, W. E. B. *The Souls of Black Folk*. Chicago: A. C. McClurg & Co., 1903.

Ellis, Trey. *Platitudes*. New York: Vintage Contemporaries, 1988.

_____. *Right Here, Right Now*. New York: Simon & Schuster, 1999.

_____. "The New Black Aesthetic." *Callaloo* 38 no. 2 (Winter 1989): 233-243.

Ellison, Ralph. *Invisible Man*. New York: Random House, 1952.

_____. "The Little Man at Chehaw Station." John Callahan, ed. *The Collected Essays of Ralph Ellison*. New York: Random House, 1995.

_____. "Notes for Class Day Talk at Columbia University." John Callahan, ed. *The Collected Essays of Ralph Ellison*. New York: Random House, 1995.

Espada, Martin. *A Mayan Astronomer in Hell's Kitchen: Poems*. New York: W. W. Norton, 2001.

Farley, Christopher John. *Before the Legend: the Rise of Bob Marley.* New York: Amistad, 2006.

400 Years without a Comb, directed by Willie Morrow (RBG Library Videos), DVD.

Harold and Maude, directed by Hal Ashby (1971; Van Nuys, CA: Paramount Home Video, 2000), DVD.

Hurston, Zora Neale. *Their Eyes Were Watching God.* New York: J. B. Lippincott, 1937.

James, Darius. *Negrophobia: An Urban Parable.* New York: Citadel Press, 1992.

Jones, Lisa. *Bulletproof Diva: Tales of Race, Sex and Hair.* New York: Doubleday, 1994.

Lethem, Jonathan. *You Don't Love Me Yet.* New York: Doubleday, 2007.

Marked for Death, directed by Dwight H. Little (1990; Chatsworth, CA: 20th Century Fox, 1998), DVD.

Marx, Leo. *The Machine in the Garden: Technology and the Pastoral Ideal in America.* New York: Oxford University Press, 1964.

Mastalia, Francesco and Alphonse Pagano. *Dreads.* New York: Artisan, 1999.

Menon, Ramesh. *The Ramayana.* New York: North Point Press, 2001.

Mercer, Kobena. "Black Hair/Style Politics." *New Formations* No 3 (Winter 1987): 33-54.

Mithen, Steven. *The Prehistory of the Mind: The Cognitive Origins of Art, Religion and Science.* London: Thames & Hudson, 2003.

Morrison, Toni. *Tar Baby.* New York: Alfred A. Knopf, 1981.

_____. *Song of Solomon.* New York: Alfred A. Knopf, 1977.

Murray, Albert. *The Hero and the Blues.* Columbia: University of Missouri Press, 1973.

_____. *South to a Very Old Place.* New York: McGraw-Hill, 1971.

Nelson, Jill. *Straight, No Chaser: How I Became a Grown-Up Black Woman.* New York: Putnam, 1997.

Rattray, R.S. *Ashanti.* Oxford: Oxford University Press, 1923.

Reed, Ishmael. *Mumbo Jumbo.* New York: Doubleday, 1972.

Roth, Philip. *The Human Stain.* New York: Houghton Mifflin, 2000.

Senna, Danzy. *You Are Free: Stories.* New York: Riverhead, 2011.

She's Gotta Have It, directed by Spike Lee (1986; Beverly Hills, CA: Metro-Goldwyn-Mayer, 2008), DVD.

Walker, Alice. *Anything We Love Can Be Saved: A Writer's Activism.* New York: Ballantine, 1997.

White, Shane and Graham White. *Stylin': African-American Expressive Culture, from Its Beginnings to the Zoot Suit.* Ithaca: Cornell University Press, 1998.

Whoopi Goldberg: Live on Broadway, directed by Thomas Schlamme (1985; Santa Monica, CA: Lions Gate Entertainment Corp, 1991), VHS.

Acknowledgments

With much love and affection to my family: Bertram and Dolly, Pamela and David, Jordan and Garnet.

Thank you: Judithe Andre; Black Style seminar, Fall, 2011, at the University of Richmond (Charlotte Brackett, Katherine Bull, Gyra Chan, Mallory Fryc, Ryan Harrity, Stephen Minnich, Amani Morrison, Elon Ng, Gabrielle Pound, Mary Richards); Ronald Brown; John Callahan; Junot Diaz; Patrick Doyle; Sean Egan; English Department of the College of the Holy Cross; Paige Fogarty; Amina Gautier; Robert Gross; Katie Hardy; Cate Harkin; William Hobbs; Jo Hutcheson; Agymah Kamau; Trent Masiki; Roberto Mighty; B. Eugene McCarthy; Kelly McDonald; Reginald McKnight; Kimberly R. Moffitt; Rachel Pittman; Paige Reynolds; Lindsay Robinson; Danzy Senna; Eve Shelnutt; David Stevens; David Wright; Richard Yarborough

Special Thanks: Yvonne Beaulieu-Bullock; Daryl Cumber Dance; Trey Ellis; Alex French; Carmen Gillespie; Destiny LeVere; David Shields; Michael Sturgeon

Very Special Thanks: Elizabeth Outka

And depthless love and gratitude to my wife, Valerie. I don't know what I'd do without you.

About the Author

Bert Ashe is an associate professor of English and American Studies at the University of Richmond. He lives in Virginia with his wife.